THINKING
IN AN
EMERGENCY

AMNESTY INTERNATIONAL GLOBAL ETHICS SERIES

General Editor: Kwame Anthony Appiah

In December 1948, the UN General Assembly adopted the United Nations Declaration of Human Rights and thereby created the fundamental framework within which the human rights movement operates. That declaration—and the various human rights treaties, declarations, and conventions that have followed—are given life by those citizens of all nations who struggle to make reality match those noble ideals.

The work of defending our human rights is carried on not only by formal national and international courts and commissions but also by the vibrant transnational community of human rights organizations, among which Amnesty International has a leading place. Fifty years on, Amnesty has more than two million members, supporters, and subscribers in 150 countries, committed to campaigning for the betterment of peoples across the globe.

Effective advocacy requires us to use our minds as well as our hearts; and both our minds and our hearts require a global discussion. We need thoughtful, cosmopolitan conversation about the many challenges facing our species, from climate control to corporate social responsibility. It is that conversation that the Amnesty International Global Ethics Series aims to advance. Written by distinguished scholars and writers, these short books distill some of the most vexing issues of our time down to their clearest and most compelling essences.

Our hope is that this series will broaden the set of issues taken up by the human rights community while offering readers fresh new ways of thinking and problem-solving, leading ultimately to creative new forms of advocacy.

FORTHCOMING AUTHORS:

Rory Stewart and Gerald Knaus

Richard Thompson Ford

Jonathan Wolff

John Broome

Sheila Jasanoff

Martha Minow

Philip Pettit

John Ruggie

ALSO BY ELAINE SCARRY

The Body in Pain:
The Making and Unmaking of the World

Resisting Representation

On Beauty and Being Just

Dreaming by the Book

Who Defended the Country?

Rule of Law, Misrule of Men

THINKING
IN AN
EMERGENCY

Elaine Scarry

W. W. NORTON & COMPANY

NEW YORK LONDON

For information about permission to reproduce selections from this book,
write to Permissions, W. W. Norton & Company, Inc.,
500 Fifth Avenue, New York, NY 10110

For information about special discounts for bulk purchases, please contact
W. W. Norton Special Sales at specialsales@wwnorton.com or 800-233-4830

Manufacturing by Courier Westford
Book design by Iris Weinstein
Production manager: Devon Zahn

Library of Congress Cataloging-in-Publication Data

Scarry, Elaine.
Thinking in an emergency / Elaine Scarry. – 1st ed.
p. cm. – (Amnesty International global ethics series)
Includes bibliographical references and index.
ISBN 978-0-393-07898-5 (hardcover)
1. War and emergency powers. 2. Abuse of administrative power.
3. Emergency management–Government policy. I. Title.
JF256.S33 2011
363.34'561–dc22

2010049522

ISBB 978-0-393-34058-7 pbk.

W. W. Norton & Company, Inc.
500 Fifth Avenue, New York, N.Y. 10110
www.wwnorton.com

W. W. Norton & Company Ltd.
Castle House, 75/76 Wells Street, London W1T 3QT

3 4 5 6 7 8 9 0

for Eva Scarry

1921–2010

librarian, grammarian, best teacher, sweet friend

CONTENTS

PREFACE

As a child growing up in the high hills of South India, Rae Langton used to walk to school side by side with a friend. So did all the other children. They could be seen each day moving two by two along the pathways in a long undulating line, chattering, laughing, holding hands. The children called it walking "in croq" because collectively they moved like a crocodile toward their shared destination.

Overnight this practice changed. Walking in croq was suddenly prohibited. The flow of schoolchildren could still be seen each day as they made their way across the terraced hillside, but now they moved in single file or in atomized clusters of two or three.[1]

Walking two by two in a line was construed to be a form of assembly, and the right of assembly—as well as India's other fundamental rights—had been suspended as of midnight, June 25, 1975. The mountain town of Ooty is 2,000 kilometers from the seat of government in Delhi, but Prime Minister Indira Gandhi's act had entered directly into the texture of the schoolchildren's lives. The children of this town were not privy to the severe abuses and injuries that would now take place: the cutting of electricity to opposition newspapers, the imposition of severe censorship once the electricity was restored, the detaining of thousands of persons without charge and without release of their names, the involuntary sterilization of many who were detained.[2] But despite their separation from the site of grave injury, the children had a physical sign in their environment that some profound change had just come about.

The abridging of rights and laws more often lacks any sensory manifestation. Persons who are not themselves directly injured often do not even know that any substantive change in the laws has taken place. If at the moment that President George W. Bush secretly authorized torture the residents of the United States had been required to begin walking in single file, the enormity of the legal change might have been easier to grasp. They would be concretely aware that their shared legal universe had changed, and perhaps they would suspect that somewhere somebody else might be paying a heavy price for the change.

What about the profound legal change that comes about once a country acquires nuclear weapons that allow the executive of that country to kill many millions of people in a foreign land? If at the moment the change was initiated the residents of that country had been henceforth required to walk backward wherever they went, they would be steadily aware that a major alteration had occurred. The sustained discomfort of walking backward would surely trouble them on their own behalf. It would almost as surely prompt them to worry about the enormity of the far-heavier price that some unseen population might eventually pay for the mysterious change.

It is not the case that any of the eight nuclear nations have required their populations to walk backward physically, even though that is precisely what those populations have been asked to do legally, morally, and spiritually. Nuclear weapons—their possession, threatened use, or use—reenact on a vast scale the structural features of torture. Both torture and nuclear weapons inflict their injuries without permitting any form of self-defense; both inflict their injuries without obtaining any authorization from their own legislatures or populations; both starkly nullify even the most minimal requirements of a contractual society; both destroy the foundational concept of law.

Thinking in an Emergency is a reminder of what in the nuclear age we sometimes seem to have forgotten: that we have both the responsibility *and the ability* to protect one another, both within the boundaries of our own nations and across national boundaries. Once we hold in front of our eyes the landscape of actual emergencies—as the central chapter of this book asks us to do—we can recognize the deep principles of mutual protection that consistently appear, whether in the act of a midwife in Zambia trying to save a newborn with CPR, a commune in Saskatchewan building a raft to rescue stranded villagers, or an entire national population in Switzerland working in concert to uphold their commitment to "equality of survival." We can and ordinarily do retain our ability both to think and to act in emergencies, and should not be misled by governments into believing that the speed of modern life requires that populations step aside and stop thinking while larger and larger arsenals are accumulated whose only purpose is to injure.

We need to turn to this work of mutual protection. If we are late in beginning, we are not yet too late.

THINKING
IN AN
EMERGENCY

Chapter One

THE SEDUCTION
TO STOP THINKING

I n his mid-twentieth-century book on *Constitutional Dictatorship*, Clinton Rossiter predicted that the atomic age would
soon be governed by emergency rule and a solitary executive figure.[1] He was right. A recent report by the Geneva Center
for the Democratic Control of Armed Forces reviews the governance structures of the earth's eight nuclear states: the United
States, the United Kingdom, France, the Russian Federation,
China, Israel, India, and Pakistan. All eight have ceded control
of nuclear weapons to their presidents or prime ministers; all
eight have permitted their legislative assemblies and their citizenry to disappear.[2]

There are, of course, distinctions among the eight nuclear
weapons states. Of 22,600 weapons held worldwide, the United
States and Russia hold 21,600 of them.[3] The countries vary in
their readiness to fire: both China and India keep their warheads
"unmated" to the delivery vehicles;[4] the United States and Russia together keep 2,000 ready for launch day and night. Strategic
policies vary: India is committed to a "second-use only" policy,[5]
whereas the United States and Britain have a first-use policy (the

United States adopted a first-use policy shortly after acquiring a nuclear weapon, formalized the policy as Presidential Directive 59 in 1980, and defended the legality of firing nuclear weapons first at the International Court of Justice where, in 1995, seventy-eight countries petitioned to have nuclear weapons declared illegal). The number of people who will initiate any launch also varies from country to country: in the United States, the president issues the order to launch alone;[6] in Pakistan, three people—the prime minister, the president, and a third unidentified person—must act in concert to launch a weapon, as is also true in Russia where the president, the defense minister, and the chief of the general staff share control over the release codes.[7]

While these and other differences are important, what unites the eight countries should be kept steadily in view. Each has the capacity to kill millions of people; each has placed that capacity in a small number of hands; each has bypassed the distributional structures that characterize democratic governance; and each has a population that could bring its own national laws (as well as international laws) to bear on ridding itself of both the nuclear weapons and the legal deformations those weapons cause.

Legal scholars have shown that by the end of the twentieth century many countries have come to live in the state of "chronic emergency" that Clinton Rossiter predicted, with more and more powers ceded to the country's president or prime minister. Hans Born, the author of the Geneva study, judges that among the eight nuclear states, the United States has a strong chance of reestablishing democracy both because of various constitutional provisions and because of a robust civil society. Given this democratic potential, it is revelatory to see how saturated with emergency rule this particular nation has become. Supreme Court attorney and constitutional scholar Jules Lobel calls attention to a Senate report acknowledging that by the 1970s "470 statutes existed delegat[ing] power to the executive over virtually every aspect of American life," presidential power that since then has increased, appearing in presidential control of drug wars, civilian transportation, and civilian nuclear plants.[8] Astonishingly, even the constitutionally specified arrangement for presidential succession has itself been replaced by two separate lines of presidential succession, determined not by constitutionally legal procedures but by private councils within the executive.[9] Counterparts of many of these legal deformations can be found in the other nuclear states. For example, both Russia and France have set up lines of succession that diverge from the constitutionally mandated sequence;[10] in Britain, two deputies are appointed, one of whom can launch the weapons if the prime minister is not available to do so.[11]

In the United States, the dissolution of law in the second half of the twentieth century accelerated in the twenty-first. In the first eight years of the new century, the claim of emergency and the momentum toward unconstrained executive power became increasingly legible, with a presidential office that sanctioned the practice of torture, detention without charge, widespread surveillance of its citizens, and a private mercenary army answerable only to the president.[12] The first in this list—the practice of torture—carried the United States into the deepest region of war crime. The international and national prohibition on torture is not just one law among many but a foundational prohibition underlying the larger framework of laws.

As these many acts indicate, the overall shift in government across the last sixty years has entailed setting aside distributional mechanisms in favor of centralized ones, setting aside democratic arrangements in favor of monarchic ones, setting aside constitutional provisions for nonconstitutional ones.

Among these monarchic and nonconstitutional arrangements, the most grave are the arrangements for nuclear weapons.[13] In the United States, nuclear weapons and the strategic doctrines for their use have bypassed two major provisions of the Constitution: the prohibition on initiating war without a formal declaration of war by the full legislative assembly (Article I, Section 8, Clause 11), and the prohibition on an executive military force that acts independently of the population's authorization and consent (the Second Amendment). Together, these two provisions place a large brake on the attempt to go to war; they stipulate that the United States cannot begin to injure a foreign population unless reasons can be given that are so persuasive that they survive scrutiny and testing by both the national assembly and the population at large. These provisions were meant to ensure that military authority would be distributed to the whole population. In turn, that distribution was meant to guarantee that the country would remain a democracy, not a tyranny. By setting aside these constitutional provisions, the country gives up the form of government it should rightfully treasure and protect. We give it up whether or not the weapons are ever actually fired. And if they are fired? We then exterminate another population, as well as millions upon millions of other living creatures.

All along, the people of the United States have had the legal procedures to prevent this from happening. Why didn't we use them? We still have those legal procedures. Why don't we use them now? The existence of nuclear weapons endangers all the populations of the world. They are truly what in earlier centuries was meant by the legal principle *Quod omnes tangit,* "that which touches all." That sentence has a second half: *Quod omnes tangit, ab omnibus decidetur,* "That which touches all requires everyone's agreement."

This book looks at the way a spurious invocation of emergency in the nuclear age has acted on the people of the world to make us surrender our powers of resistance and our elementary forms of political responsibility. The book will also show that, correctly understood, we collectively and thoughtfully address many forms of emergency conditions, and do so by honoring—not abandoning—procedures that are legal, open, widely understood, and carefully prepared in advance of the crisis to make possible a democratic, not a dictatorial, response. We need to reacquire our responsibility for our own governance. If it is perilous to cede our collective political responsibilities to any single authority under normal peacetime conditions, it is far more perilous to do so when vast injuries to the earth's people, and to the earth itself, are at stake.

THE CLAIM OF EMERGENCY

The implicit claim of emergency is that all procedures and all thinking must cease because the emergency requires that 1) an action must be taken, and 2) the action must be taken relatively quickly. It is odd to set the first of these, the requirement that an action be taken, in opposition to deliberative thinking. The unspoken presumption is that either one can think or one can act, and given that it is absolutely mandatory that an action be performed, thinking must fall away. But at least one whole genre of thinking—what Aristotle called "deliberation"—has no other function than precisely to enable the taking of actions. In *De Anima*, he differentiates thinking that is directed toward an apprehension of "what is," which he calls "perception" and elsewhere "contemplation," from a form of thinking directed toward decisions about "whether to do one thing or another,"[14] which he designates "deliberation."

Even if we now move back from the specific genre of deliberation to the more encompassing act of thinking, it is clear that the claim is an odd one: the call to suspend thinking is precisely a call to suspend governance, whether self-governance or the governance of the polis. How integrally governing and thinking are coupled is most rapidly displayed by recalling that our major political treatises tend always to be written by people who have also written treatises about how we think. *The Republic* and *The Laws*, themselves saturated with observations about cognition, were written by that same Plato who wrote about the mind in the *Timaeus*, *Theatetus*, and *Phaedrus*. Aristotle's *Politics* exists side by side with writings such as *Prior Analytics* and *Posterior Analytics*, as well as writings on cognition: *De Anima, Sense and Sensibilia, On Memory, On Dreams*. Thomas Hobbes's *Leviathan*, centrally a work about the social contract, opens with chapters interrogating the nature of the mind—"Of Sense," "Of Imagination," "Of Reason, and Science"—an interrogation also present in *De Corpore*, an early exemplar of the computational theory of mind. John Locke wrote not only *The Second Treatise of Government* but the *Essay on Human Understanding* and again, *Conduct of the Understanding*. John Stuart Mill wrote *On Liberty* and *Considerations on Representative Government*; he also wrote *A System of Logic* and an essay "On Genius." This insistent coupling reflects the intimate association between understanding governance and understanding understanding. As we shall see, the two are nearly a single merged subject.

The first of the two seductions to giving up thinking in an emergency—the argument that emergency requires an action—is not, then, a very creditable one. The second seduction—the argument that the action must be done soon—is more problematic because more plausible. Aesop tells a tale about a young boy who is drowning.[15] He calls to a nearby huntsman for help. The huntsman, disapproving of the boy's rashness, begins to lecture him. The boy calls out: "No. Save me now. Lecture me later." At the end of Aesop's tale, which lasts only as long as the sentences just recited, the moral seems to be that in an emergency there is no time for thinking or deliberating, certainly not for lecturing. Now, this would be an odd piece of advice for Aesop to give, since the fables collectively constitute a small treatise on emergency thinking—a set of lectures to those who are drowning, or were, or might someday in the future be, drowning. And in fact, true to his own emergency primer, the explicit moral we now come to in the postscript to the story of the drowning boy repudiates the huntsman's posture of reprimand (while simultaneously reenacting it), for it counsels that one ought not to get into a situation that licenses anyone else to reprimand you. The fable, then, provides two rules about emergency. The first rule of emergency thinking is that that one ought not to get into one; the huntsman delivers this rule. Aesop backs it up one more step: one ought not to get into a situation that makes it appropriate for someone to remind you that the first rule of emergency is not to get into one. There is surely a third rule at work here: whatever happens, keep talking.

The second great seduction to giving up thinking in an emergency, then, the argument that the speed of emergency requires action without thought (the drowning boy's position), is displaced in Aesop by the advocacy of cognitive acts that have the power to anticipate and eliminate the conditions of emergency. Aesop calls for thinking that preempts the emergency. Rather than emergency bringing about the end of thinking, thinking should bring about the end of emergency.

But how is this to be done? The basic assumption during peacetime is that the world stays the same and persons change. The stability of the world acts as the background for the display of our changes, our circuitous thoughts, our contemplative digressions. But in an emergency this is inverted: the world is changing more quickly than we can change. Baudelaire's poem about a swan misplaced in Paris suffering the conditions of exile, "trailing his white plumes on the raw ground,"[16] provides an image for those displaced by emergency: Andromache bewildered by the loss of Hector and the Trojan War, an African immigrant searching the Parisian sky for the palm tree of her home. In an emergency, the mind is in exile like Baudelaire's swan, "with his frenzied gestures, ridiculous and sublime." The thinking mind is this big beautiful creature, helpless in exile from the conditions of its own thought.

THE MIND IN EXILE IN EMERGENCY

Aesop's recommendation to remain coherent in an emergency is difficult to carry out. Thucydides gives the classic account of the dissolution of conventions during the plague of Athens. No medical therapy helped, he writes. "Nor was any other human art or science of any help at all. Equally useless were prayers."[17] Soon no one even attempts remedy. Thucydides designates this immobilization the most "terrible thing of all"; when people realize they have the plague, "they would immediately adopt an attitude of utter hopelessness, and, by giving in in this way, would lose their powers of resistance."[18] People become indifferent to "every rule of religion or of law," disregarding even funeral ceremonies, adopting "most shameless methods" of disposing of the bodies. Thucydides calls this a "state of unprecedented lawlessness."[19] The dissolution of laws, customs, and religious ceremonies entails at its heart a dissolution of language: "words indeed fail," says Thucydides. Aesop's dictum to "keep talking" is lost among all the other lost rules.

The portrait of cognition Thucydides gives is consistent with the more familiar experience of emergency in everyday life. Language disappears. Words are replaced by loud noises, crude sirens, harsh horns—one-syllable sounds that act as placeholders for language until it can return. The few words that remain tend to be the minimalist vocabulary of counting, as in the rules for cardio-pulmonary resuscitation ("ONE one thousand, TWO one thousand, THREE one thousand") with its 15:2 ratio for a rescuer acting alone, its 5:1 ratio for two rescuers acting as partners. So fragile is our hold on emergency language that—as in Aesop's well-known tale about the boy who cried wolf—there must exist special rules for keeping it intact, special constraints on invoking the vocabulary of alarm lest we exhaust its too-easily-exhausted powers before the actual problem arrives. This fragility is also registered in the special legal categories that have been designed to protect and regulate emergency language: fighting words, dying words, crying fire in a theatre.[20]

One might conclude from historical portraits of actual catastrophes (whether in ancient Athens or today) that human beings lose their social and political structures in an emergency not simply because they have suddenly been subjected to an asocial and anarchic framework but because they are, in their own deepest impulses, asocial and anarchic. Certainly Thucydides is often understood to be illustrating this account of humanity.

But it is not at all clear that this conclusion is warranted. A Canadian quarterly publication called the *Emergency Preparedness Digest* reviews a constant stream of actual and hypothetical emergencies (grain elevator fires, laboratory disease outbreaks, tornadoes, chemical spills, ice breaks in spring, tsunamis in all seasons); and it analyzes existing civil defense procedures, hypothetical rescue strategies, communications problems whose solutions range from meteor-burst warning systems (radio signals relayed across the continuous sequence of meteors available in the heavens) to the establishment of community agreement about the meanings of a siren "yelp" as distinguished from a siren "wail." The portrait repeatedly presented here is that people in emergencies—or at least Canadians in emergencies—are neither asocial nor anarchic. We would be social if we knew what gestures or actions to perform, and even without that knowledge, we are often diffusely social. So, too, we would be responsive to leadership if a clear site of authority were visible. The absence of direction may come from the fact that there is no one present, or instead from the fact that there are too many people present; Quebec Civil Defense finds in some emergencies between "200 and 300 persons on the scene from various organizations responsible for emergency measures,"[21] itself providing the grounds for the type of crowd panic described by Elias Canetti in his classic book *Crowds and Power*.

It is in spite of our socialness and lawfulness that the framework of norms and laws dissolves, not because of an inherent wish to be free of such constraints. In the absence of any mental stays, one may become vulnerable to the most rigorous stays, orders issuing from outside. The psychology of this susceptibility is unapologetically elaborated in Antonin Artaud's writings on the immobilization of the theatrical audience in his Theatre of Cruelty, where the play assumes a potentially dictatorial power over the audience, stunning them into full attention that has no object other than the spectacle. Artaud, who claims the plague as an analogue for the theatre, is clearly fascinated by Thucydides.[22] The single most influential sentence in Thucydides's account is the surrender to hopelessness that deprives the population of resistance. The goal of the emergency spectacle, says Artaud, is to bring about "a genuine enslavement of the attention."[23] "I propose then a theatre," he writes, "in which violent physical images crush and hypnotize the sensibility of the spectator seized by the theatre as by a whirlwind of higher forces."[24] If Artaud's audience were equipped with the procedures from Canada's *Emergency Preparedness Digest* (and somewhere in its pages there must exist an article on what to do if one finds oneself at a play by Artaud), or if they had the 901,000 days a year of active practice that the Swiss population collectively has for its fallout shelter system, or even if they had practiced the "scrum" gesture that (for many decades) every scout who received a Fireman's Badge had to be able to perform, they would have the capacity for resistance.

Artaud is important because he unashamedly displays the theatre director's own monarchic motives for emergency decrees. A political leader who brings about chronic emergencies may have these same motives: to stun the mind, to immobilize, to bring about a genuine enslavement of attention. But he is unlikely to author a political treatise on this subject, for it would arm the reader with the very scepticism that enables resistance.

As one scans across the plagues of Thucydides and Artaud, across the tidal waves and grain elevator fires in Canada, and the Swiss vision of unspecified war, three alternative political descriptions of the population recur: the first is immobilization; the second is incoherent action; the third is coherent action. The first alternative is one in which a population is incapable of initiating its own actions and highly susceptible to following orders imposed by someone else, as illustrated in Artaud's account of audience passivity in France, or in Hannah Arendt's account of the obedience of Eichmann in Germany, or in the notorious Milgram experiments in the United States where subjects willingly inflicted electric shock on other people if instructed by a scientist to do so. The other two alternatives entail the performance of an action in which some level of self-authorizing agency remains. What the rest of this book focuses on is the extraordinary role played by habit in shaping these two alternative forms of self-authorization. In an emergency, the habits of ordinary life may fall away, but other habits come into play, and determine whether the action performed is fatal or benign.

The seduction against thinking in an emergency comes, as we have seen, from two sources: first, from a false opposition between thinking and acting; second, from a plausible (but in the end, false) opposition between thinking and *rapid* action. Now a third, equally potent, form of seduction becomes visible: the acts of thinking that go on in emergencies are not recognized by us as acts of thinking. We misrecognize them. More precisely, we correctly recognize the presence of habit in these mental acts but incorrectly conclude that habit is incompatible with, or empty of, thought. We are therefore willing to set these mental acts aside. Our derisive attitude toward habit prevents us from seeing the form of thinking embedded in these cognitive acts and hence makes us willing to give up, or set aside, the most powerful mental tools that stand ready to assist us.

The first two seductions entail an overt repudiation of the act of thinking. This third one is, on the surface, just the opposite. Out of a deep regard for thinking, in the name of thinking, we set aside practices that—because they correctly appear as habit—are *incorrectly* taken to be removed from the realm of thought. We need to see that not only mental habits but their codified counterparts, procedural pathways and legal rules, are deeply compatible with the most rigorous forms of thinking. Far from being set aside, they need to be respected, revered, and practiced.

THE ROLE OF HABIT IN EMERGENCY

The habits of everyday life, as Thucydides makes clear, often fail to serve in an emergency.[25] But in the absence of our ordinary habits, a special repertoire of alternative habits may suddenly come forward. It is not the case that ordinary life is habitual and emergency life is nonhabitual. Both coherent and incoherent emergency actions appear to have their source in habit.

The habits that suddenly surface may have been culturally

received without our self-consciously aspiring to acquire them. A friend in Philadelphia was alarmed when she opened the oven door and saw a mouse. More accurately, she was stunned not to see the mouse but to hear the sentence that came out of her mouth: "Eek. A mouse." There are many serious illustrations of this same phenomenon. In a book called *Running Hot*, an ambulance emergency worker describes the difficulty of obtaining and transmitting to the hospital accurate medical information, because by the time the ambulance crew arrives at the home, fifteen people may be moving anxiously about the room. So, too, at the hospital: the information the ambulance team gives to the physician or nurse receiving the patient at the door may not reach the physician who then treats the patient in an interior room. As both the portrait of ambulance work and many other forms of emergency work make vivid, coherent deliberative acts are made extremely difficult by seriatim thinking—by a sequence of temporally or spatially distinct locations for the various stages of examination, inquiry, and decision-making. The alternative to seriatim structure is an assembly structure where all contributors to the emergency decision are co-present in a single space and a single time. Governmental structures designed to guarantee the most careful and thought-laden decision-making have this assembly form; thus, in the United States the constitutional requirement for a congressional declaration of war (Article I, Section 8, Clause 11) and for jury deliberation (Fourth Amendment) seek to insure that information, rather than being passed from person to person, is examined under the pressure of consistent attention across participants.

A seriatim structure is, of course, a necessity in the case of a patient whose injury or illness originates in a location distinct from the hospital or treatment center. The condition of the patient being transported by the ambulance is likely itself to be in a state of rapid change. Often, once the ambulance begins its run, a person who seemed to have been unconscious in the home may turn out not really to be unconscious. "Patients have no basis for judging what is appropriate," writes Donald Metz.[26] "They have been known to pretend they were unconscious until loaded into the ambulance, because they did not know what was expected of them and so adopted a stereotyped role of the 'ambulance patient.'" Contained in this account is *no* implication that the patient has been faking, or melodramatizing the situation, or inappropriately seeking sympathy; indeed, the person is often gravely injured or ill and, in addition, deeply mystified about what to do. Because the cultural image of an ambulance patient is one of unconsciousness, the person may simply absorb that cultural habit and mime unconsciousness.

Many stories about emergency are precisely about the appropriateness or the inappropriateness of the habits that surface during them. Aesop tells the story of a little donkey who carries a heavy burden of salt one day and finds that when he wades through the river, the salt dissolves and his burden disappears. So the next day he again carries his heavy load into the river. But this time he is carrying sponges (which absorb the water) and he drowns. Aesop has many other tales about applying the wrong habit or instead, by foresight and preparation, applying the right one. It is because a set of given actions will either accelerate the emergency or instead bring it to a halt that carefully chosen emergency preparations must be put in place. Far from being structureless, a crisis is an event in which structures inevitably take over. The only question is whether the structures will be negative or positive.

Because this book will go on to speak about philosophic assessments of habit, it will be useful to set before the reader four concrete instances of emergency preparation that depend, for their essential design, on the willful instilling of deeply formed habits in advance of the catastrophe. It will be helpful to keep these concrete pictures in front of the mind throughout the rest of the analysis. The fact that the four models come from widely different contexts suggests that a key feature cuts across and unites many genres of emergency preparation.

Chapter Two

FOUR MODELS OF
EMERGENCY THINKING

FIRST MODEL: CPR

The first model is cardio-pulmonary resuscitation. Classic CPR procedures consist of a rigid set of rules about counting. Almost all actions are accompanied by a number, and the counted actions are paced by the inclusion of filler words: "ONE one thousand, TWO one thousand, THREE one thousand." The distribution of the rescuer's efforts between two locations, the chest and the mouth, is also numerically specified: thirty compressions at the chest for every two breaths at the person's mouth. If the rescuer has a partner, fifteen acts are carried out at the chest for every two that the other rescuer performs at the mouth. The few pieces of language that are not numerical are as terse as numbers and, again, rigidly specified. Because, for example, CPR is physically demanding and might have to go on for a long period (ten minutes, twenty minutes, forty minutes), the two rescuers may need to change positions; this change is signaled by the person at the chest substituting the word "change" at the place where one would normally say "four": "ONE one thousand, TWO one thousand, THREE one thousand, CHANGE one thousand, FIVE one thousand." A breath is now given by the rescuer at the mouth and the two rescuers change locations.

The procedures for CPR confirm a feature of habit that is often cited in critiques of habit, its rigidity, while at the same time vividly illustrating the mistake those critiques make when they attribute to rigidity a robotic (or automaton-like) lack of thought. Built into those 30:2 and 15:2 ratios is a deep knowledge about the number of times a minute the heart must pump to support the body and the minimum amount of oxygen that must be in that pumping blood to keep the tissue—and in particular, the brain—unharmed; built into those ratios also is a deep knowledge about the difficulty of thinking clearly if a child's or a friend's or a stranger's heart has suddenly stopped beating. The acts, far from being thoughtless, are thought-laden; they are designed to carry out the actions of breathing, circulating, and thinking during the period while those three internal actions are in a state of suspension. Further, the very fact that the rescuers know precisely what to do increases the chance that they will retain their ability to think clearly. The procedures are so efficiently internalized that mental space is left over for addressing additional complicating problems.

CPR conflates the extraordinary with the ordinary. It enables someone who has died—or who will within a very few minutes be dead—to turn around and step back onto the path of life. Given its connection to reanimation, it is appropriate that historians have glimpsed the earliest traces of the aspiration for CPR in ancient Egypt and ancient Hebrew, both civilizations receptive to the miracle of reanimation. The discovery of an ancient

Egyptian mouth-opening instrument, believed to be connected to the cult of the dead, has prompted the thesis that the practice of artificial respiration may have begun five millennia ago.[1] The Hebrew scriptures also provide possible precedents, such as the description in 2 Kings of Elisha the Prophet bringing a child back to life: "He placed himself over the child. He put his mouth on his mouth, his eyes on his eyes, and his hands on his hands, as he bent over him. And the body of the child became warm . . . Thereupon, the boy sneezed seven times, and the boy opened his eyes."[2] Despite these and other fascinating precedents, false starts, and successful first-second-and-third steps across many centuries and geographical regions, the actual invention of CPR is usually assigned to the year 1959, when five scientists—Peter Safar, James Elam, James Jude, Guy Knickerbocker, and William Kouwenhoven—brought together their two independent lines of research on breathing and circulation.[3]

Are its miraculous powers of reversal certain, or even likely? CPR only sometimes brings the person back to life, and only some of those who recover go on to live a long time. But that sentence is equally accurate with the twice-repeated "only" removed: CPR sometimes brings the person back to life; some of those who recover go on to live a long time. One study of a rural hospital in Kenya looked at 114 children who were given CPR in a two-year period from 2002 to 2004: eighty-two had stopped breathing (and were therefore a short time away from their hearts stopping as well); thirty-two had suffered arrest of both lungs and heart.[4] All were severely ill from one of three causes: malaria, extreme malnutrition, or septicemia. Most were younger than six years old.[5] Of the eighty-two children who had stopped breathing, twenty-five began to breathe again after being given CPR; of those twenty-five, eighteen lived long enough to be discharged from the hospital. Of the thirty-two children whose heart and lungs had both stopped, five regained breathing and heartbeats after CPR. Although none of these five lived long enough to be discharged from the hospital, the temporary return of breath and circulation would have given them a chance for longer life had it been possible to reverse the dire sickness each had—as may, someday in the future, be possible. Of the 114 children, then, thirty regained life: twelve very briefly, eighteen long enough to become healthy and leave the hospital.

The survival rate following CPR is tracked at the Kilifi District Hospital in Kenya and at hospitals in many other countries in the world precisely because the expectation is that it should be, and will with study become, higher. Indeed, the survival rate for the Kenyan children who had suffered respiratory arrest represented a significant increase over the survival rate a few years earlier.[6] Similarly, a 2003 study of Nigeria's Lagos University Teaching Hospital found that during 2,147 operations in a one-year period, thirteen patients suffered cardiac arrest. The average age of the patients was thirty.[7] All thirteen were given CPR but only five survived. The authors of the study report these figures to urge the repair of the two major causes for the unacceptable level of survival: extreme loss of blood (a problem that can be solved through a better hospital blood bank) and inadequate conformity to the International Guidelines on administering CPR, issued in 2000, again in 2005, and most recently in 2010.[8]

The potential miracle of CPR grows out of the non-miraculous fact of repetition—repetition carried out on three levels. First, as noticed earlier, the act itself is comprised of a set of repeated actions. In the case of Lagos University Teaching Hospital, the mean duration before the person regained spontaneous circulation was twenty-five minutes; thus the person or persons compressing the heart repeated that action more than 2,500 times (100 beats per minute for twenty-five minutes). In the case of the children in Kenya, no child given more than fifteen minutes of CPR survived. Even this much briefer duration would require 1,500 compressions of the child's chest and 100 breaths.[9] Infants are given cheek-puffs of breath, rather than the deep, forceful, double breath given to adults; the presses on the center of the sternum are done with two fingers backed by the strength of the arm, rather than, as with adults, two overlapping hands and the weight of the rescuer's full upper body.

Second, both the initial acquisition of the skill and the maintenance of the skill entail repetition and practice. The goal of the initial training is to impress a small set of facts into the learner's mind so vividly that they might, at that moment, seem indelible. The brilliantly designed 1959 handbook on artificial respiration— *Resuscitation of the Unconscious Victim: A Manual for Rescue Breathing*, co-authored by Peter Safar and Martin McMahon— provides an example. The tiny, bright yellow book, eighty pages long and as big as one's hand, ends by singling out in its penultimate paragraph one fact in particular without which all other facts will fail: "We believe that the teaching of the 'head tilt, chin up' position will save more lives than the teaching of any method of artificial respiration." Almost fifty years later, the 2005 International Guidelines still specify the importance of the "head tilt, chin up" position as the best way of assuring a clear airway.

A person who is unconscious often has his head falling forward with his chin "sagging" toward his chest. In this position (and even in the normal position with the chin perpendicular to the chest), the back of the tongue completely blocks the passage from the throat to the airways leading to the lungs. Only if the head is arched back and the chin is pulled up so that the throatline is taut will the airway fully open and the rescuer's breaths begin to reach his lungs. This fact is artfully enfolded into the 1959 manual's verbal analysis *thirty-one* times (in one two-page section it recurs seven times).[10] In addition, it is visually represented with twelve illustrations of the correct position of the victim's head, throat, and neck: ten are full-page, two are half-page. The ostensible purpose of many of these drawings is some additional instruction, but the "head tilt, chin up" position continues to be vividly rendered. The use of stark line drawings is crucial, for bodily learning—the ability of viewers to reproduce in their own bodies what is depicted in the visual field—happens much more rapidly with sketches and cartoons than with photographs or paintings.[11]

Six of the twelve illustrations incorporate another key instruction—"watch the chest"—either by stamping those three words onto the visual diagram or by a dotted line going from the rescuer's eyes to the person's chest. Once the chest rises, one takes one's mouth away from the person's mouth, so that air will be expelled before the next breath is given—a principle restated thirteen times in the verbal text. Can one, after reading the handbook, ever forget these two rules: "head tilt, chin up" and "watch the chest"? Safar and McMahon assume the answer is yes. The handbook advises practicing every six months, the same interval that today, fifty years later, is still advocated.[12]

One 2009 study of neonatal resuscitation in delivery clinics in Lusaka and Ndola, Zambia, found that the performance capacity of college-trained nurse midwives (who already had an average of sixteen years of experience) more than doubled after being given explicit training in CPR. Before training the midwives carried out many acts correctly, such as warming the infant sufficiently, but did not know aspects of resuscitation such as the depth of the chest compression that would give the infant the best chance of survival. Despite a great improvement after training, the study also found that the abilities of the midwives fell off markedly after six months; in fact, their skills were only slightly better than they had been prior to training.[13] Worldwide, four million newborns die each year, one million of them from the arrest of heart and lungs; and since neonatal resuscitation is "simple, inexpensive," and "readily available," the study urges retraining in CPR every six months (and introduces the possibility that it should be done as often as every three months). The Nigerian study cited earlier similarly urged that all anesthetists in the Lagos University Teaching Hospital participate in "organized simulations" and "continuing training," and pointed out that the International Guildelines explicitly counsel periodic retraining. The Kilifi, Kenya, study also specifies that the learning achieved in any pediatric advance life support course is "*short-term* knowledge" only and that "recertification is important if the concepts . . . are to be retained."[14]

The consequence of failing to refresh knowledge every six months has been observed in countries all over the world. An unannounced 2010 test of CPR in the Hospital of Brigham and Woman's in Boston, Massachusetts, revealed that only the physicians and nurses whose specialty was emergency medicine showed complete conversancy with CPR; even those physicians and nurses working in the cardiology sections of the hospital performed substantially below the recommended standard.[15] The *learning* and *relearning* of CPR, like the *act* of CPR, is built on repetition.

The existence of International Guidelines, protocols, and handbooks carries us to the third level of repetition. Knowledge of CPR must be distributed across millions of people in every country in order to be effective. It must become not only an individual habit but an earth-wide habit. Concrete instances of the practice of CPR in hospitals have been given above because accurate statistics can be more easily gathered in the controlled situation of a hospital than on the street or in widely dispersed homes or workplaces. But most instances of cardiac arrest do not occur in the hospital; three-quarters of them happen in the home or at work or on the street.[16] Even the time it takes for an ambulance to arrive may be too much time. Sixty seconds after a person stops breathing, his oxygen level begins to drop; it continues falling rapidly. While many organs can survive a brief interruption of oxygen, the brain begins to suffer damage three to five minutes after it stops receiving oxygen.[17] Both the chance of survival and the chance of surviving without brain damage therefore depend on rapid response. The Lagos Teaching Hospital study found that the chance of survival tripled if CPR was begun in the first minute of cardiopulmonary arrest. If everyone in the hospital knows CPR, no time is lost running through the ward to find the one person who does know it. Studies of the street similarly emphasize the advantage of a small time window. One study of bystander CPR found that the survival rate was greater than 18% if the CPR was started in under two minutes and 12% if over two minutes.[18]

Only if knowledge of the practice is widely disseminated can the practice itself be practiced. Distribution is therefore not just a tertiary attribute of CPR; it is the heart of what it is. Physician Mickey Eisenberg's historical study of CPR, *Life in the Balance: Emergency Medicine and the Quest to Reverse Sudden Death*, is of necessity as much about the strategies of distribution as it is about medical research. That is in part because the founders of CPR themselves saw distribution as the key to its lifesaving powers. James Elam's medical research, for example, provided crucial evidence about the life-giving quality of expired air; though the oxygen level of breath is lower during exhalation (16%) than inhalation (21%), it provides enough oxygen to allow the blood of the subject to reach (and hold) a 100% saturation level.[19] He also demonstrated that the then current forms of manual respiration delivered *zero* oxygen. But while continuing his research, he also met on Saturday mornings with Buffalo fire and ambulance squads and gave them theatrical demonstrations of the oxygen levels in the competing forms of assisted respiration, all registered on a giant dial which could be read by everyone in the room. When he moved to Baltimore, he (along with Peter Safar) constantly lobbied the Army, the Red Cross, and the National Research Council to endorse and thereby assist the distribution of the new procedure. He also made a film, *Rescue Breathing*.[20]

Like Elam, Peter Safar from the outset coupled medical research with distribution. His 1959 manual described above, *Resuscitation of the Unconscious Victim*, was simultaneously published in the United States, Canada, and the Commonwealth Nations of Great Britain.[21] Safar's co-author, Martin McMahon, was the captain of the Baltimore fire and ambulance service, a partnership that began when Safar gave regular classes to firemen who in turn trained others.[22] Crucially, it was this attempt to carry the results outside the exclusive domain of physicians and onto the streets that in turn suddenly accelerated the medical research itself, for it was fireman McMahon who was responsible for bringing together the two independent avenues of research, one on assisted respiration (Safar and Elam), the other on assisted circulation (Knickerbocker, Kouwenhoven, and Jude) which might have remained stranded from one another, as they had been throughout earlier decades and centuries.[23]

Blood needs to be laden with oxygen, but blood also needs to be (in Eisenberg's well-chosen word) "propelled" throughout the body. Conclusive evidence that circulation could be accomplished by massaging the chest—massaging it without cutting open the chest and acting on the heart directly, as originally attempted—was the work of James Jude, Guy Knickerbocker, and William Kouwenhoven at Johns Hopkins University Hospital, who also determined the best location, direction, and speed of the compressions. Crucial to the dissemination of their findings were two 1960 journal articles, the first of which, in the *Journal of the American Medical Association*, carried it to the international medical community, and the second of which, in *Reader's Digest*, carried it to the public at large. *JAMA* reported that of twenty patients who suffered cardiac arrest in the hospital, fourteen had survived with the assistance of heart compressions lasting as little as one minute or as long as sixty-five minutes. The youngest person was two months; the oldest, eighty. But while the *JAMA* article focused on the work of the top research scientists, it simultaneously made clear that the procedure belonged not to physicians and nurses but to the people everywhere: "Anyone, anywhere, can now initiate cardiac resuscitative procedures. All that is needed is two hands."[24] *Reader's Digest*—which in 1960 had an international circulation of 23 million[25]—carried the news much further. It chose to describe not in-hospital cases but an out-of-hospital case, narrating the story of the first person (as the magazine framed it) to be "snatched from death by a layman using the closed-chest method."[26]

Bystanders who give CPR greatly increase the chance that the person suffering cardiac arrest will survive. A 1994 study of New York City, for example, found that bystanders who gave CPR on average initiated it within one and a half minutes of the heart attack and that the people they helped had a three times higher chance of survival than those not receiving help.[27] A 2005 study of Los Angeles similarly found that bystanders doubled the chance of a person surviving, and tripled the chance if the bystander was present at the moment the person first collapsed.[28] A 1998 study of large areas of urban and rural Sweden again found that bystanders doubled the chance of survival.[29]

Yet what is being doubled and tripled in all these geographies is a very low survival rate to begin with. Without bystander help, fewer than one in one hundred (0.8%) survive in New York; almost three in one hundred (2.8%) survive with bystander help; thus the overall New York average is one person in one hundred.[30] Los Angeles and Chicago[31] similarly have a one-in-one-hundred survival rate, as does Johannesburg, South Africa.[32] Sweden's overall rate is five people in one hundred, due to the much shorter time it takes for the ambulance to arrive and for defibrillation to begin. Shortening the time to defibrillation and the arrival of professional paramedics is key to increasing the numbers: traffic congestion is credited with causing the slow arrival time of New York ambulances (11.4 minutes); ambulances in need of repair and sections of the city lacking street names and numbers are credited with the fact that so few patients in Johannesburg live long enough to be eligible for defibrillation.[33] Key, too, to higher survival is raising the number of bystanders who feel competent to assist. The number is already high,[34] but increasing it still further will contribute to better survival rates, as citizen education in other regions of the United States and other countries of the world has shown.[35]

A country in which one has a greater chance of surviving an out-of-hospital cardiac arrest is Japan, where 1.4 million people are trained in CPR every year. One study tracked bystander intervention in Osaka during an eight-year period (1998–2006) when residents were learning CPR and ambulance personnel were for the first time permitted to use a defibrillator without a physician present. As a result of citizen training, the cases of cardiac arrest in which bystanders delivered CPR rose from 19% to 36%. The time that elapsed before CPR was initiated shortened, as did the time it took to contact the emergency service. The overall survival rate in Osaka rose to 12%.[36] The 12% survival figure can be contrasted with the 1% survival figure in New York, Chicago, and Los Angeles, and the 5% survival rate in the Swedish cities of Stockholm, Gothenburg, and Malmö and surrounding rural regions. Most studies give—in addition to overall survival rate—the much higher survival rate for a subset of cardiac arrest that begins with ventricular fibrillation: in this category the overall survival rate in the three American cities was 5%, in Sweden 9.5%, and in Osaka 16%.

Equally striking evidence of the importance of population-wide training is the help bystanders in Kyoto gave to the 5,170 children who suffered out-of-hospital cardiac arrest during a two-year period between 2005 and 2007.[37] The children's heart attacks were brought on by internal causes such as heart problems, respiratory diseases, and tumors, or by external causes such as hanging, drug overdose, and drowning.[38] Bystanders gave CPR to 2,432 of the children, almost half of the total number (47%).[39] The study differentiates between those bystanders who used classic CPR—both chest compression and breathing—and those who used compression alone, and found that the first had greater life-sustaining powers and better neurological outcomes.[40] But it also stresses that *any* version of CPR more than doubled the child's chance of not only surviving but doing so with a minimum of neurological damage.

While, then, CPR is a habit structure built on repetition—repetition within the act, repetition in the initial acquisition and subsequent maintenance of the practice, repetition of the practice across millions of people in every country of the world—it has high levels of thinking and research built into it. Indeed, Columbia University president Jonathan Cole's recent book about brilliant discoveries carried out by American research universities cites the 1959 invention of CPR as an instance of why the United States—and by implication, every other country—should continue to support universities.[41] True of the original discovery of CPR, so too the ongoing refinement of our understanding of the conditions under which it best works requires huge investments of intellectual labor, whether—as the studies cited above illustrate—at the University of Johannesburg, the Lagos Teaching Hospital, or the thirteen hospitals and medical centers in Kyoto, Osaka, Senri, and Seattle that contributed to the eight-year Osaka study.

This constant research also means that the practice is continually reviewed and refined when evidence indicates the procedures should change. Classic CPR—with chest compressions given at the rate of 100 per minute, a 30:2 ratio of compressions to breath if one is acting alone, a 15:2 ratio if one is acting with a partner—is still the recommended procedure for professional caretakers, for bystanders giving CPR to children and infants, and for confident, well-trained bystanders giving CPR to adults. But the international guidelines now suggest that if one is an untrained or an unconfident bystander, or a bystander hesitant to place one's mouth in contact with an adult's mouth, one can deliver only the chest compressions.[42] Much more research is needed to confirm the benefits of this shift in recommended procedure.

Some recent studies of bystander assistance during adult cardiac arrest show that (as with the Kyoto children) classic CPR is more beneficial than compression-only. But other studies suggest compression alone may be equally effective. Several explanations have been given for this puzzling fact. First, compression-only is much easier for an untrained bystander; the instructions for compression-only can be given by a telephone dispatcher to a bystander more easily than can the steps of classic CPR. Carrying out one part of CPR correctly may be as, or more, effective than doing both parts haphazardly. It is also the case that the chest compressions must be given rapidly and forcefully at 100 beats per minute; interrupting that action for too long an interval to give breaths can jeopardize the momentum of the compressions. Finally, a reluctance to place one's mouth on a stranger's mouth may make the bystander carry out both actions with less commitment and passion than are needed; it may even make bystanders hesitant to begin. The 2005 guidelines called for much more research on this question, whose results affected

the next set of guidelines issued in November 2010.
2008 advisory from the American Heart Associ~
mended "hands only" ("compression only") CPR. ⌐
Call to Action for Bystander Response," indicates the hope th~
this recommendation will recruit more people into the practice
of CPR.[43]

• • •

This first emergency procedure looked at here—CPR—is one that
focuses on individuals. The arrest of heart and lungs (whether in
a newborn or in an adult) happens one person at a time; so, too,
the acquisition of the knowledge and skill embedded in CPR
happens one person at a time. The next section will turn away
from the individual to emergency procedures that are collective
in nature and that enlist the efforts of small assemblies of people.
We will see the part played by habit in emergency procedures
that together constitute civil society.

But before turning away from CPR, it is useful to take note
(even in the midst of this highly individualized act) of the part
played by civil society—municipal fire departments, schools,
churches, the International Red Cross, the American Heart
Association, the National Research Council, Boy Scouts, Girl
Scouts—in encouraging the distribution of the rescue practice
across the world's population. Eisenberg's history of CPR provides striking evidence of the part played by civil society at every
stage of the long endeavor to discover the best set of steps for
restoring breath and heartbeat. The Amsterdam Rescue Society
was formed in 1767 in order to recommend procedures for resus-
citating those who had drowned; in response to Amsterdam's
act, the cities of Venice and Milan began similar societies in 1768;
in 1769 the city of Hamburg required a reading in all churches of

the best steps to follow to assist "the drowned, strangled, frozen, and those overcome by noxious gases"; Paris started its rescue society in 1771; St. Petersburg, in 1774; London, in 1774. What is today known as the Royal Humane Society in England began as the Society for the Recovery of Persons Apparently Drowned when physicians in London read the reports of successful resuscitations in Amsterdam.[44]

Recommending an anthology of procedures (some of which would still today be credited, and many others wholly discredited), these eighteenth-century societies not only saved lives but helped create the wide aspiration to find the way to, in effect, restore the heart and lungs to their habitual actions. Here is the fourth level of habit embedded in CPR: the human heart beats thirty-one million times a year.[45] How could it suddenly "forget" how to do this? CPR is a procedure in which a conscious understanding of the pumping motion of the heart is directly relayed to the heart by the rescuer's hands. After what may be as little as one minute or as long as sixty-five minutes, the heart remembers and reacquires its habitual motion.

SECOND MODEL: MUTUAL AID CONTRACTS

A second model of emergency action is provided by the arrangements for mutual aid in the dispersed communities on the plains of Canada's Saskatchewan province. Small constellations of towns and farms sign an explicit social contract promising mutual aid, as is audible in the language of the contract of the Quill Plains Mutual Aid Area: "each party to the agreement will assist any other party to the agreement in the event of a disaster."[46] This language, or a close equivalent, is repeated in many of the other social contracts from the Saskatchewan province, such as that of the Battlefords Mutual Aid Area. The contracts vary in size. The Quills Plain contract binds together three towns and four rural districts, each in itself sparsely populated (approximately 700 people) but together becoming 5,000. The Battlesford contract brings together 23,000 residents.[47] The signing of these local contracts predates their formal authorization by the Legislative Assembly of Saskatchewan which in 1989–90 passed "An Act Respecting Emergency" whose Article Eleven stipulates that local communities "may enter into agreements" with other communities for "mutual aid" and the "pool[ing] of resources."[48] The provincial government by this act endorses and facilitates what the local communities have in many cases already brought into being.

The power to declare the emergency is also local: Article Twenty of the Emergency Planning Act specifically gives to the "local authority" the right to make the declaration and stipulates that if, because of the crisis, the members who together constitute the local authority are dispersed, some one member can make the declaration on behalf of the local authority as a whole, thereby setting into motion a series of legal powers and paths of financial support.

On July 3, 2000, for example, the eighty-house village of Vanguard suffered a torrential downpour of rain. In this part of the Saskatchewan prairie, the annual rainfall is eleven inches. But on this single evening—between 4 p.m. and midnight—over thirteen inches of water fell; its impact on Vanguard was amplified by the fact that the tiny village is situated at the bottom of a valley and thus received additional water flowing in from surrounding hills.[49] Streamflow records for nearby Notuku Creek had been kept for over sixty years by a hydrometric station. Streamflow is measured in cubic decameters (dam³): a decameter is ten meters, a cubic decameter is one thousand cubic meters. The *annual* discharge of Notuku Creek averaged 28,500 dam³ with a monthly figure of zero in the dry periods of each year. During this one storm, the discharge was 73,000 dam³, by far the highest level it had ever reached.[50] A few minutes after midnight, the deputy mayor and another council member met by candlelight to put the formal declaration of emergency into effect.[51] Next morning at daybreak the full council met at the mayor's house.

The Vanguard storm was an intensified version of a storm that was hitting a 1,700-square-kilometer region. With 353 million cubic meters of water reaching the ground, it was "the largest eight-hour storm ever documented on the Canadian prairies."[52] The rain was accompanied by other sources of terror: between 6 p.m. and 7 p.m., 1,051 strokes of lightning were recorded (and in the storm as a whole, four times that number), and immediately southwest of Vanguard a band of hail fell that produced "100% crop damage." But by far the greatest problem was the water. The lower bands of the storm over Vanguard consisted of air that three days earlier had been "on-the-ground" in a corridor of farm states from Texas up to North Dakota absorbing moisture from "rapidly growing agricultural crops"; the upper bands of air had three days earlier been "near ground-level" in the fertile central valley of California, again absorbing moisture from the fast-growing crops. Once the storm reached Vanguard, it became "anchored" to that spot by a strong wind blowing from the north that prevented the storm itself from continuing its northward-moving direction.[53] The Saskatchewan plains often receive severe weather but usually that weather sweeps rapidly by; on this night, it stayed fixed in place for many hours.

Vanguard was now an island surrounded by water. How then could people from the outside who wanted to help get in? A small Hutterite community ten kilometers to the south, Cypress Hutterite Colony Farm, immediately built a barge and carried in fifty volunteers, that first day and on the days following.[54] A farmer with a small plane landed on a patch of available ground to lift out those who were stranded and needed to leave. The residents (all of whose homes had two to eight feet of sewage in the basements) were offered accommodations in a small, nearby college that was empty for the summer; but the residents declined to abandon their homes.[55]

For three months (July, August, September) Vanguard residents had no water. Individual wells and the village reservoir were contaminated with E. coli bacteria and with the herbicides that had been put on the fields in the preceding four weeks. Though no pesticides had been recently used in the fields around Vanguard, waters rushing in from other regions brought this third form of contaminant as well.[56] A bottled-water company in the town of Swift Current brought in the first truckload of water, which ten bottling companies around the province continued to deliver without interruption, and without cost, during the three months.[57]

Supplying Vanguard and the immigrant volunteers with food was a complex, but apparently (for the people of Saskatchewan) not a difficult, problem to solve. Communities such as Swift Current and Regina—separated from Vanguard by 72 kilometers and 260 kilometers respectively—were among the many that provided the residents with food day after day.[58] The backbreaking work of clearing and bleaching the basements, and digging a deep pit to bury and treat the contents of the storm-ruined abattoir, was carried out by residents and neighboring communities. Communication was carried out during this period by a series of letters hand-delivered to each house—for example, urging the residents not to drink the water even if it appeared clear, and later providing instructions on the procedure for clearing and testing the wells. The letters were delivered by high school graduates who a day before the storm had returned to their single-building K–12 school for a July 1 Canada Day town reunion.[59] This house-by-house form of communication (rather than anonymous media announcements) was singled out as key in all the after-action reports: "Concise information is needed quickly and people may not absorb this in the normal manner. Hand delivery is the recommended option."[60]

The Saskatchewan mutual aid contracts specify procedures for determining lines of authority and communication. Equally important, the contract may explicitly require that lists be made of materials (such as welding equipment or maps or trucks) that individual owners have agreed to contribute during any crisis.[61] The compilation of such a list itself acts as a rehearsal; it requires the community to think through a starkly specific set of questions about the tools required in a flood, in a mudslide, in a fire, in a chemical spill, in a plow wind, in a tornado, and to designate the actual location where each tool exists and the person who will bear the responsibility for bringing it to the site.

Early in the morning of April 18, 1990, a grain elevator caught fire in Naicam, a town of 900 residents and a member of the Quill Plains Mutual Aid area. A grain elevator (which typically holds 168,000 bushels of grain) is itself a cooperative structure in which many farmers pool their produce.[62] Historians have attributed Saskatchewan's inclination toward progressive politics (the province originated Canada's Progressive Party and was the first region in North America to have a health care system) to its early habits of cooperative ownership of grain elevators.[63] In the late nineteenth century, these structures were privately owned, but by 1911 they had become associations; by 1975, almost all of them (79%) were farmer-owned rather than privately owned.[64] The Naicam grain elevator is shared by three hundred farms in the region. On this day in 1990, the burning elevator itself became the beneficiary of another voluntary association, the Quill Plains Mutual Aid contract.

Within five minutes of the fire report, the Naicam all-volunteer fire truck arrived; a truck from Spalding (11 kilometers away) arrived in fifteen minutes; a truck from Melfort (54 kilometers away) arrived in fifty-five minutes with an aerial ladder that would prove decisive during the course of the day.[65] Forty minutes later, as the winds changed and the fire became more threatening, a request for the Watson fire truck (33 kilometers away) was issued. Three fans of branching telephone calls brought waves of food and volunteers with shovels during the nine-hour fire fight.[66]

As was true at Vanguard, any major problem in these prairie towns usually, at some point, involves a question of water. With four fire trucks together pumping 10,000 liters a minute, the problems of exhausting the water supply began to loom, even with the water shut off in parts of the town. Thus, two hours into the fight a convoy of twenty farm trucks with large and small water tanks—the large-capacity trucks already designated for this job in the Quills Plain Mutual Aid contract, the small trucks spontaneously volunteering—began a steady tour to and from Round Lake five kilometers from the town.[67] Because the mayor had declared an emergency at the time the request to the trucks was made (9:15 a.m.), crews were legally able to barricade the entire roadway so that the trucks could proceed without interruption or danger.[68] By 11:15, the town well still had 391,500 liters remaining, but at 10,000 liters a minute that would have permitted only thirty-nine minutes of water had there been no farm trucks assisting.[69]

Equally concrete as the plan for confronting fires is the elaborate Saskatchewan design for evacuation and billeting. Communities that agree to be "receiving communities" keep their houses stocked with materials to accommodate those evacuated; the registry of houses is reviewed twice a year; one receiving community practiced once a month, and at the end of two years had a major simulation in which people were housed and fed for two weeks.[70] The Saskatchewan town of Kindersley devised a billeting plan that would accommodate 1,500 persons. Rather than testing it with an evacuation exercise, they arranged for a week of indigenous games in December 1994 and used the billeting arrangements to house 1,500 athletes. The arrangements for housing and food were so well distributed that only a few additional people were needed to register the guests and keep them informed.[71]

Such exercises, not only in Saskatchewan but in other Canadian provinces, are forward-looking rather than backward-looking; they are designed not only "to test" the procedures that are already in place, but "to design" systems that will be increasingly supple in their response. One exercise in Nova Scotia, for example, confronted that province with a day-long

hypothetical emergency that consisted of 415 separate inci-
dents spiraling out of hurricane-force winds, freezing rain, and
fire. The test, involving both civilians and military, drew on
the resources of seventeen municipalities, six companies, and
twelve federal departments. The exercise revealed military
reliance on acronyms that civilians could not decipher; it also
made visible the need to design smaller mutual aid areas, to
decentralize lines of authority, and to enhance the powers of
local municipalities.[72]

These varying levels of mental rehearsal enable participants to
become competent and confident. Equally important, if there are
politically problematic procedures, those come to the attention
of the community long before they are put into actual practice.[73]
For example, the Saskatchewan Emergency Planning Act has a
number of provisions which permit the suspension of ordinary
democratic procedures once a formal declaration of emergency
has been made by either the national or the local government. It
allows immediate conscription; it allows entering a house without a warrant; and it includes provisions for both prohibiting
and requiring movement, thereby restricting the ordinary right
of entry and exit (as was true when the road between Round
Lake and Naicam was sealed off to all vehicles other than farm
trucks carrying water). But because the procedures have been
subjected to public scrutiny, additional clauses have been added
that place restrictions on the emergency powers, both by limiting
the number of days an emergency declaration can last and by
requiring compensation for damage done during the emergency.

However problem-laden such provisions are, they should be
contrasted with the situation of a country where no civil defense
procedures have been specified, or where procedures have been

specified by one branch of the government but are not known to the population at large because (as in the United States)[74] no public discussions and practice of civil defense ever take place.

As noticed above, the Saskatchewan social contracts are sometimes highly specific in their content, detailing the piece of equipment which any one person will be relied on to bring. The necessity of this kind of specification is amplified by the distances separating members of the mutual aid contract; one might otherwise drive 15 kilometers to the site of a problem only to find that the tool one has brought has already been carried there by several other rescuers and that some other highly needed tool can only be supplied by circling back home in a 30-kilometer round trip during which the calamity will continue to unfold. While this specificity may prove crucial, even more crucial is the fact of regularly working and planning together, whatever the content of that work or planning session.

This principle, vividly at work in Saskatchewan, was dramatically demonstrated in the immediate aftermath of the Kobai earthquake that in 1995 killed 6,000 residents of Japan and left 350,000 people homeless. The government—as media from Japan and from around the world soon noticed—was immobilized by "ineptitude" and "jurisdictional disputes," whereas 1.2 million volunteers moved in with speed and precision, donating not only their labor but $1.6 billion to the devastated districts.[75] According to Robert Pekkanen, the surge of spontaneous assistance is correctly attributed to the remarkable fact that Japan has 300,000 small neighborhood groups (or, to be precise, 298,488). As one study of Yokohama makes clear, the association—though on average comprising between 100 and 300 households—may be as small as seven homes or as large as three thousand.[76] These neighborhood associations do not mentally rehearse how to clear rubble after earthquakes; but they do habitually clean parks, maintain roads, clear streams, and repair street lamps. They do not practice attending to the injured and homeless, but they do regularly support children's groups, youth groups, and the elderly. They do not organize disaster relief, but they do routinely organize neighborhood celebrations of festival days.[77]

One might call these practices "habits of mutual aid," or one might instead use the designation Alexis de Tocqueville long ago assigned to them: "habits of the heart."[78] In his travels through America in the nineteenth century, Tocqueville was astonished by the practice of voluntary association that he saw in people "of all ages, all conditions, and all disposition" organized around every conceivable subject, "religious, moral, serious, futile, general or restricted, enormous or diminutive," collectively attempting to carry "to the highest perfection the art of pursuing in common the object of their common desires."[79] Although not so extravagantly diverse, the voluntary associations in Japan certainly take varied forms: urban, suburban, rural, neighborhood associations (*chounaikai*), local retailers' associations (*shotenkai*), "self-government associations" in high-rise apartment complexes and labor unions (*jichikai*).[80] The response of the Japanese neighborhoods to the Kobai calamity is consistent with Tocqueville's description of the effect of voluntary associations: "Feelings and opinions are recruited, the heart is enlarged, and the human mind is developed only by the reciprocal influence of men upon one another."[81]

As observed earlier, the question is not *whether* habit will surface in an emergency (it surely will) but instead *which* habit will emerge, and whether it will be serviceable or unserviceable.

Japan's governmental bureaucracy certainly had its own well-practiced, deeply entrenched habits, but these turned out to be incapacitating while the "habits of the heart" practiced by the neighborhood associations turned out to be enabling. As it happens, these groups are almost entirely independent of the government, so much so that Japan has often been described as a country that suppresses civil society. Unlike many democracies, Japan does not grant to voluntary associations a tax-exempt status, or give them the virtually free mailing privileges that equivalent groups elsewhere receive, or grant them legal recognition as incorporated "persons" that would let them receive donations or gifts. The spectacle of 1.2 million volunteers putting themselves at risk (despite the fact that none of them were covered by insurance) led to a countrywide demand for a major modification in Japan's relation to its own civil society. A 1998 Non-Profit Activities Law now allows such voluntary groups much greater freedom from bureaucratic oversight than they had earlier, and confers legal recognition on them.[82]

While, then, habit is often seen as a phenomenon unresponsive to "change," habits inevitably come into play when people face world-changing events such as torrential storms, fires, and earthquakes. In turn, the habits which prove beneficial in an emergency may also bring about—as in the case of Japan's Non-Profit Activities Law—significant changes in formerly unyielding governmental structures.

The compatibility between mutual aid compacts and the necessity of confronting change has been documented in many other countries. In Africa, voluntary associations—what one scholar calls "economies of affection"[83]—existed long before colonial rule and the emergence of states. These "long-standing informal solidarities" sometimes retained the same form when the population confronted rapid urbanization, and elsewhere gave rise to new forms.[84] During the third, fourth, and fifth decades of the twentieth century, for example, thousands of rural residents in West Africa migrated to Lagos, Nigeria, and Accra, Ghana–cities that had no provisions for assisting them if they were sick, injured, unemployed, orphaned, or distressed by the dislocation of their sudden move. The practice of voluntary association, which many of the migrants carried with them from their hamlets or villages, provided for pooling of resources that covered the cost of illness, disability, funerals, court appearances, newly arriving babies, the formation of schools, and scholarships for promising children.[85] By 1956, for example, almost 17,000 people in Accra belonged to at least one voluntary association, most of them comprised of thirty to one hundred people but sometimes much smaller or much larger. The society membership was sometimes based on the village from which the migrants came (*association d'originaire*) but other times based on common interest or form of work.[86]

Regularly addressing individual emergencies, these societies "were also in the habit of providing a lump sum to each member in rotation"[87] by establishing a carefully designed system to facilitate savings. For example, market women in the Ghanaian association called Nanemei Akpee (Society of Friends) provided working capital for one another through their weekly meetings; each week, each member made a carefully recorded contribution to a collective sum which was given to one member, until all members had taken a turn, after which the rotation would begin anew. Named "rotating credit associations" by Clifford Geertz,[88] this form of mutual aid society exists not only throughout West

Africa but throughout the world, in places such as China, Vietnam, India, and England.[89]

In Africa—as in Saskatchewan and Kobai—nature continues in the late twentieth and early twenty-first centuries to provide countless hazards that must be protected against. A form of association visible in the twenty-first century that is continuous with long practice is the assistance farmers give one another in places such as the Oromo region of eastern Ethiopia. Here "seed insecurity" is a large problem. Most farmers grow a form of sorghum that requires eight or nine months to mature; if too much or too little rain falls during this time, they need to reseed, using the slow-growing cultivars if the season is still early and the more rapidly growing, but less nutritious, forms if the season has progressed. Each farmer saves seed—storing it "above the cooking fire" or "in an underground pit"—but often there is not enough for multiple sowings; then farmers rely on the seed stores of neighbors (as well as the marketplace if they have money). The voluntary associations are not family-based: during 1998, for example, no farmer reported receiving seed from kin; neither did any farmer receive seed from an NGO source.[90] Because "mutual aid associations are common among the Oromo, and norms stress generosity with seed," large volumes of seed move from farm to farm, leading to great diversity in the plants.

This long-standing cooperation among eastern Ethiopian farmers has many analogues, such as the practices of mutual aid among farmers in Zimbabwe that, even during the severe famine of 1982–84, helped peasant farmers survive. During the drought, women often had to walk 15 kilometers each way to obtain water; teachers in the Matabeleland and Masvingo provinces reported children fainting in the classrooms; the Ministry

of Health reported that 70% of the children in these
were undernourished; more than a third of the cattl/
as in the case of eastern Ethiopia in the early 2000s, it wa.
tary association rather than biological association that was reliec
upon. As the "drought deepened" over the course of one year,
the number of households which could no longer feed themselves rose from 16% to 56%; but people did not go to family
members for help. Assistance given by relatives (who often live
at a distance) was never higher than 9% and fell to lower levels as the drought grew more severe.[91] The voluntary associations, in contrast, grew stronger as the famine grew more severe
despite the fact that the sharing of oxen, a central practice of the
associations, was diminished by the death of so many of the animals.[92] Mutual aid not only enabled the people to survive but, as
Michael Bratton writes, led to the "amazing" fact that "peasant
families grew and sold more maize in the first five years of independence [1980–85] than during the previous years."[93]

What in Africa or Japan or Canada is the effect of the mutual
aid contracts and voluntary associations on the larger population, the population outside the boundary of the association
itself? We have seen that the members themselves are, without
question, beneficiaries of these associations. But do these "habits
of the heart," "economies of affection," and "norms of generosity" spill outside the associations, affecting other people and
even the state as a whole? The examples above all suggest the
way the "norms of generosity" overflow from the interior to
the exterior. In Saskatchewan, the Hutterite village that made
the barge for rescuers trying to reach Vanguard, and the town of
Regina that contributed to the food, are not formal members of
the town's voluntary association. In the mutual aid communities

of eastern Ethiopia, 50% of the farms which provided seed to their fellow association members also gave seed to farms outside the association.[94] In Japan, the neighborhood groups who assisted the earthquake victims of Kobai became their neighbors at the moment the earthquake struck.

This same principle of transfer appears to describe the relation of civil society to the state as a whole.[95] Voluntary associations help to protect the entire population of a state because, as Tocqueville long ago stressed, they act as a safeguard, diminishing the impact the executive power of a state can have on the people.[96] A second effect (or perhaps instead, a second way of saying the same thing) is that such voluntary associations increase "the accountability" of a government to its population.[97] A third effect (or alternatively, a third restatement of the first two) is that such voluntary associations appear to address the governments of the countries in which they reside not for personal favors but for actions in the public interest.

In his widely known study *Making Democracy Work: Civic Traditions in Modern Italy*, Robert Putnam compared towns with weak and robust habits of voluntary association (such as sports clubs, community organizations, and youth groups). Citizens of towns with extensive practice of voluntary association contacted their governmental officials much less often; and when they did, the issue raised was almost always some problem of public interest. The citizens in towns with low levels of voluntary association contacted their government officers frequently, but did so to ask for jobs or personal favors (the "average councillor" in such districts receives eight to ten inquiries about personal favors every day)—almost never to call attention to an issue affecting the public good.[98]

• • •

The first two examples of emergency preparation—CPR and mutual aid contracts—address hazards which usually come from nature: earthquakes, torrential rain, severe drought, fire, disease, and the fallibility of the human body that can suffer a heart attack even when the sun is shining and the ground is still. The third and fourth genres of emergency preparation—which will be looked at in the sections that follow—come not from nature but from the other profound source of hazard, the phenomenon of war. In moving to these next two forms of emergency preparation, the subject will shift from injuries decoupled from human intention to injuries that are the direct outcome of such intention. The focus will also shift from small collaborative groups (collectively called by the name "civil society") to the much larger and more unitary collective that is the nation-state.

Before moving away from voluntary associations, however, it is important to notice a feature that has so far been ignored. While our attention has here centered on voluntary associations as remedies against natural disasters, it is also the case that they have often been instigated as a response to—a way of heading off—the possibility of war. Legal scholars describe how, in the eleventh and twelfth centuries, many of the five hundred major European cities came into existence as mutual aid societies to protect the inhabitants against external sources of human aggression. The cities did not accidentally emerge. They came about through explicit acts of oath-taking and contract-making. "A solemn collective oath, or series of oaths," writes Harold Berman, "[was] made by the entire citizenry to adhere to a charter that had been publicly read aloud to them."[99]

Often called "sworn communes," "conjurations," or "com-

munes for peace," their very names memorialized the remarkable verbal process by which they had come into being. The
purpose of that verbal act was to forge a strong link between self-
governance and the diminution of injury. The founding charter
of Freiburg, for example, emphasized the guarantee of "peace
and protection."[100] The Flemish charter of Aire opened by identi-
fying the assembled persons about to take the oath as, "All those
who belong in friendship to the town," then promised, "Let each
help the other like a brother."[101] The articles of the charter for
Beauvais in Picardy began:

> All men within the walls of the city and in the suburb shall swear
>   the commune;
> Each shall aid the other in the manner he thinks to be right;
> If any man who has sworn the commune suffers a violation of
>   rights, . . . [the peers] shall do justice against . . . the offender.[102]

It is logical for clauses of the charter promising mutual defense
to be followed by clauses arranging for jury trial because such
compacts seek to diminish injury issuing from outside the city
(war or armed attack) and from inside the city (crime). One oath
for mutual assistance from the Bologna region makes the coupling explicit: the members "should maintain and defend each
other against all men, within the commune and outside it."[103]
The "communes for peace" seek to secure their members from
both sources of injury.[104]

The town's commitment to protecting its members from outside aggression by no means implied that outsiders were themselves subjected to aggressive treatment. On the contrary: Berman
writes that "immigrants were to be granted the same rights as

citizens [the right to vote, the right to bear arms, the right to a jury trial] after residence for a year and a day."[105] Before gaining those rights, the immigrant was seen as someone deserving of special care. A 1303 guild statute from Verona, one of the oldest in existence, specifies the categories of people who should be the recipients of special aid: one had the obligation to give "fraternal assistance in necessity of whatever kind," to give "hospitality toward strangers, when passing through the town," and to offer "comfort in the case of debility."[106] The mutual aid contracts and communes for peace out of which Europe's cities grew came into being in order to protect insiders and outsiders from injury—injury that could arise either from crime or from war.

It is a remarkable fact that the nation-state in social contract theory of the seventeeth and eighteenth century has almost precisely the same point of origin. The contract comes into being, as Hobbes repeatedly urged, in order "to get us out of the miserable condition of war"; and both Hobbes and Locke repeatedly stressed that protecting oneself against crime and war was at the heart of consent theory. While, then, the interaction between civil society and the state can take many different forms, it is the urge to protect against wrongfully inflicted injury that brings both into being.[107]

THIRD MODEL: THE SWISS SHELTER SYSTEM

A third extraordinary model of the place of habit in emergency preparation is the Swiss shelter system, which is shaped by three underlying assumptions. The first assumption (as the Swiss Office of Civil Defence observes in one of its widely distributed pamphlets) is that the locus of injury in any future war will be civilians. The ratio of civilian to soldier deaths jumped sharply from World War I to World War II, then jumped again in the Korean War, then jumped once more in the Vietnam War. In a nuclear war, the casualties will be close to 100% civilians.[108]

The second assumption is that a sturdy shelter system will almost certainly save the country. If an area is directly hit by a nuclear weapon, the people will die; but if, according to Swiss medical research, a weapon explodes even two kilometers away, a fallout shelter will give five hundred times the protection available outside the shelter.[109] The fallout shelter is treated in the widely distributed pamphlets as a living, breathing entity that must be continually checked and kept in sturdy working order. Over the past four decades, the shelter has been continually subjected to new forms of testing, such as the 2000–01 tests on the shelter's immunity to electromagnetic pulse issuing from a nuclear explosion or from electromagnetic weapons.[110]

The third assumption is that a democracy must guarantee "equality of survival." Any solution to the threat of nuclear disaster must therefore be distributed across the entire population.[111] This requirement for universal access to the means of survival, repeatedly stressed in the country's 2001 *Civil Protection Concept*, is anchored in Article Two of the federal constitution of Switzerland, which includes the guarantee of "equal opportunity" among the rights and liberties the constitution exists to safeguard, as well as Article 61, which assigns to the federal government responsibility for protecting the population against armed conflict.[112] "Equality of survival" was, from the outset, restated many times in the early decades of the shelter system: *The 1971 Conception of Swiss Civil Defence* lists first, among its principles,

"A place in a shelter for *every inhabitant* of Switzerland," and later reaffirms, "Equal chances of survival for all," insisting that "the same chance of survival during wartime must be offered to *all inhabitants* of our country."[113] As the word "inhabitant" indicates, the shelter system aims to ensure equality of survival to foreign residents as well as citizens.

"Equality of survival" may be a principle that is always embedded in preparations for emergency. CPR is knowable; one can learn it if one chooses. But one cannot know who will one day be the recipient of that embodied knowledge; it is there *for any one*. Even if one has been motivated to learn CPR because one has a child who is a swimmer or a brother who has a weak heart, the knowledge is not specific to that child or brother; it is available to every person whose path crosses one's own. Of the thousands of people giving bystander CPR in the studies cited earlier, many did not know the person they were helping. The booklet on artificial respiration that so successfully teaches the "head tilt, chin up" and "watch the chest" instructions was published in a year—1956—when racial relations in the United States were still deeply strained, yet it assumes that the person learning the steps is equally likely to be giving artificial respiration to a person who is black or white. The booklet specifies the places on the surface of a white person's body and a black person's body where oxygen deprivation (signaled by the color blue) will be most visible. The same commitment to "equality of survival" is true of mutual aid compacts; all participants agree that they will take on (and distribute, or equalize, among themselves) the adversity that may fall on any one member of their association. But the Swiss shelter system makes this principle of "equality of survival" astonishingly explicit and astonishingly concrete. To have carried out this principle across an entire population is a feat of civic and moral engineering.

Swiss law requires that every house have, and maintain in good condition, a fallout shelter. The "obligation to build," for many decades a Swiss requirement, is currently encoded in Article 46 of the Federal Law on Civil Protection System and Protection & Support Service, a law passed by the federal parliament on October 4, 2002, and ratified by the population on May 18, 2003, with 80.6% voting in favor. A federal requirement, the "obligation to build" is currently enforced by the cantons (the country's twenty-six states). People who do not build a shelter must pay compensation to help pay for public shelters.[114] The shelter system underwent review and revision in the 1990s and again in the early years of the twenty-first century. Almost all aspects of the original system have been reaffirmed, even though it is now hoped that the country will have a two-year lead time before armed conflict—much less time than the time required to build the shelters but enough time to restock them.[115] In addition to the use of shelters in wartime, their use for natural disasters and epidemics—phenomena with less lead time—has been stressed since the 1990s and continues today.

In addition to the shelter requirements, Swiss law assigns specific obligations to its male citizens beginning at the age of twenty and continuing until the age of forty, an upper age that can be increased to fifty or reduced to thirty-five depending on the parliament's assessment of the likelihood of armed conflict.[116] Participation by female citizens and foreign residents is voluntary.[117] The law requires conscripts and volunteers to practice approximately four days a year.[118] Article 36 of the Federal Law on Civil Protection specifies a yearly refresher course of two to seven days, in addition to the two to three weeks of original training (Article 33) and two weeks of advanced training every fourth year (Article 35). In 1988, for example, the Swiss citizenry collectively devoted 901,000 days to rehearsing their individual assignments; in 1998 (when world tensions were lower), 600,000 days.[119]

Any Swiss man can, when asked, specify a highly precise task. One friend in Zürich, for example, is on the Committee for Special Objects. He is required during practice days to go into a particular church in Zürich, gather the altarpieces and all the statues of the saints, including the statue of Saint Roch with the accompanying statue of Saint Roch's dog who in turn holds in his mouth a Eucharist wafer. Saint Roch protects against plague because in his own life he moved among plague-stricken people distributing medicine and food. The dog first began to accompany the saint when the saint himself had the plague; the dog brought him bread each day. In caring for the Zürich statue, the man or woman assigned this task enacts the very principle of protection the statue celebrates. Further, in saving any one precious object, what is preserved is not only that object but the population's link, through that object, to many kindred objects outside of Switzerland, which may or may not survive a nuclear war. Transnational as well as national culture is at risk. Artifacts depicting Saint Roch reside in Zürich, but they also reside in Venice (the paintings by Jacopo Tintoretto and Bernardo Strozzi in the Scuola of San Rocco), in Marseille (Jacques-Louis David's painting in the Musée des Beaux-Arts), in Budapest (Alessandro Bonvicino's painting in the Szépmüvészeti Múzeum), in Toronto (Jan Miel's painting in the Art Gallery of Ontario), in Philadelphia (Giovanni Battista Tiepolo's painting in the Museum of

Art), in Sarasota (Bernardino Luini's painting in the State Art Museum of Florida), as well as in hundreds of towns and villages throughout the world that contain carved and painted depictions of the saint by unknown hands.

The civil defense conscript assigned to this Zürich church carefully wraps each artifact (including the ceramic wafer) and carries it to a specified shelter. At the end of several days, he carries each object from its shelter back to the church, unwraps it, dusts it off, and restores it to its original position. The Swiss believe that preserving a population means not just keeping individual residents free from physical injury but keeping intact networks of families and friends, and keeping intact the cultural artifacts that are precious to that population.

In addition to shelters for every person within its borders, Switzerland has built 290 shelters providing 7,416,000 cubic feet of storage for cultural objects.[120] Elaborate inventories, diagrams, and tracings have been, and continue to be, made of both movable and immovable artifacts. Preparation for protecting treasured objects includes not only securing an appropriate shelter, but also making certain that the roads, paths, and staircases to the shelters are specified. If the object is too wide to be carried up a given staircase, a new route or a new destination must be found. The Swiss laws on cultural property follow from the 1954 Hague Convention on the Protection of Cultural Property and the 1999 Second Protocol, which increased the level of protection beyond that originally provided.[121]

Switzerland has been accurately described as a "reverse Potemkin village."[122] A Potemkin village has visible façades with no actual construction behind them. Switzerland is the opposite: its shelter system has few visible structures, but inside many mountains are hidden hospitals and beneath every house is a fully stocked and working fallout shelter. Dispersed throughout the countryside are shelters for the artworks and artifacts held in common by the population that connect them to one another and to a transnational culture.

The shelter system gives Switzerland political autonomy. The Bern pamphlets many times repeat that one purpose of the shelters is to make Switzerland less vulnerable to "blackmail" or "extortion."[123] During the second half of the twentieth century and the beginning of the twenty-first, the country has had little power to persuade the superpowers to dismantle their nuclear arsenals; nor would it have been endurable to be in a permanent posture of petition, continually requesting the United States and Russia to stop speaking about sending missiles on trajectories crossing above Swiss land. The shelter system restores to the Swiss their power to affect their own destiny. It provides a form of "vertical evacuation."[124]

During these same decades in the United States, the population—without actual debate or deliberation or medical research—somehow came to the conclusion that shelters were useless and only increased the chance of going to war. No referendum (such as that in which 80.6% of the Swiss population validated the "obligation to build") was held; the decision to ignore shelters was a presidential decision. What made this outcome especially startling was that the government leaders of the United States, the very individuals who had the nuclear arsenal at their disposal, continued to spend billions of dollars on an extensive shelter system for themselves in Mount Weather in the Blue Ridge Mountains of Virginia, a man-made cavern large enough to contain three-story buildings and a lake—"a lake," as one journalist observed, "large enough for water-skiing."[125] The Federal Emergency Management Agency (FEMA) later spent $2.9 billion on a mobile shelter to supplement the fixed shelter for the president.[126]

It could be argued that the White House is a certain target, whereas the risk to the homes of the citizens is distributed over a wide area and therefore only a small risk is suffered by any one citizen. But a nuclear weapon does not "take out" a single house, whether the White House or any other house; if the White House is a likely target, all houses in Washington DC and the mid-Atlantic region should have shelters. A fully democratic arrangement might be one in which every twenty-four hours the president (on the basis of a daily lottery) were assigned a random household to go to in the event of nuclear war; the way to protect him would be—following the Swiss example—to make certain all homes were equally protected, so that wherever the lottery took him, he would have a chance of surviving.

This arrangement might even give the president a greater chance of surviving since wherever he or she was, a shelter would be nearby. Exercises designed to test White House evacuation to Mount Weather have called into question whether members of the executive branch will be able to reach the Blue Ridge Mountains, since their path to the shelter is likely to be blocked by roadways clogged with people trying to flee the East Coast. Those eligible to enter the shelter all carry a special pass which, when shown to the population, is supposed to license them to move to the front of all lines. But since most of the population has not been consulted about this arrangement, it is not self-evident that such a pass will have the hoped-for effect: during one exercise, a bus driver refused to let the cardholder jump to the front of the queue, and in another instance a presidenti; cavalcade was brought to a standstill by a farmer's truck loaded with pigs coming toward them on a narrow road.[127] The exercise of consent surfaces in unexpected ways: firing nuclear weapons does not require the population's consent; building fallout shelters for the upper echelon of government does not require the population's consent; but the president's ability to get through a clogged road *will* require the population's assistance and consent. Were there to be frequent exercises for the use of the governmental shelter, the unjustness of the arrangement would become so vivid that it would no doubt increase the pressure to eliminate the country's vast nuclear arsenal altogether, giving the United States (for the first time) a reasonable position from which to ask the rest of the world to abstain from obtaining such weapons.

Ted Gup, who has written an extensive series of investigative articles on the presidential shelters,[128] has also provided a lengthy inquiry into the secret underground shelter built for Congress at Greenbrier Hotel in White Sulphur Springs, West Virginia. One of the 12-by-15-foot doors is 19 inches thick and weighs 28 tons; the two hinges of another door weigh 1.5 tons. Since almost no congressmen knew about the shelter, they cannot be held accountable for the painful discrepancy between what the government leaders spent on their own protection and what they spent on that of the country's population.[129] Once Congress learned of Greenbrier, it renounced its access to the shelter.

In contrast to the presidential and congressional shelters, in the ten-year period between 1978 and 1988, Switzerland built 3 million new home fallout shelters (roughly 300,000 per year). In addition, they built 127 emergency operating rooms, 311 first aid stations, 892 first aid posts, and 96,000 hospital bunks.[130]

...ow has enough shelter space (including home ...utions, hospitals, and public shelters) for 114% ... Sweden and Finland currently have shelters ... and 70% of their populations, respectively; Austria has 30%; Germany, 3%.[131]

It is crucial to understand that what differentiates Switzerland and the United States is not that one country believes shelters are potentially effective and the other country believes they are ineffective. Both countries have devoted vast resources to the belief that they are effective. What differentiates Switzerland and the United States is the beneficiaries of the shelters: the population in the case of Switzerland, the government leaders in the case of the United States. Switzerland's goal is to make certain it can enact "legal equality" by making certain "every inhabitant of our country has the same chance of survival."[132] In contrast, not only was the money spent on the United States presidential fallout shelter vastly in excess of the amount spent on fallout shelters for the population (billions of dollars to protect the president, zero dollars to protect the population), it was vastly in excess of all civil defense allocated for the population, for floods, fire, hurricanes, and other catastrophes.[133] This is not gallant. Neither is it coherent.

One of two things is true. Either fallout shelters are useless, in which case neither the population nor the government should have them. Or they are useful, in which case both the population and its leaders should have them. Only a monarchic political structure could excuse an arrangement that has for its citizens no civil defense—either shelters or established practices—while lavishing elaborate structures over their own heads. The adjective "monarchic" or "tyrannic" is invoked here not merely as an expression of disapproval but as a literal designation of the form of government that results when constitutional arrangements (the just distribution of authority and risk) are dismantled. Such constitutional arrangements themselves, when adhered to, constitute the fourth example of the way custom—here, legal customs—can be formed to preempt emergencies, and will be turned to shortly.

• • •

Before turning to that fourth model of emergency preparation, it is useful to pause and contemplate the place of democracy in emergency preparation. The contrast between the all-population Swiss shelter system and the president-only shelter system in the United States uncovers a stark discrepancy between the democratic commitment of the first country and its absence in the second. This difference in the two shelter systems is indicative of a much larger difference: Switzerland's commitment to "equality of survival," shown in its shelters for all its own residents, is even more evident in the fact that the country has no nuclear weapons that put the residents of other countries at risk; the United States's lack of commitment to "equality of survival," shown in its spending all emergency money on the executive alone, is much more evident in the fact that it is by far the largest nuclear-weapons holder in the world. By this arsenal, it retracts from *all people of the world* the right of self-defense and the capacity to ensure their own survival. Needless to say, it is not just "democracy" and "democracies" that stand to be annihilated by nuclear weapons; it is all civilization, as well as the natural world that has long been the companion of that civilization. As it is civilization, not democracy alone, that is in the direct line of fire, so, too, it is civilization, not democracy alone,

that seeks to act as the guarantor of survival. This recognition is
not to put democracy aside but only to step away from it briefly,
so that when we return to it—in the fourth model of emergency
procedure below—we will better comprehend what it is we are
seeing.

Habits of emergency preparedness are much wider than, and
anterior to, democracy. It is hard, for example, to contemplate the
Saskatchewan grain elevators or the strategies for seed security in
Ethiopia or the Swiss shelters without recalling China's tradition
of "ever normal granaries," which were flourishing by the time
of the Han dynasty (206 BC to 220 AD). The grain shelters—
some round, others rectangular or square, usually on stilts high
off the ground—were intended to store grain as insurance against
famine, as well as to house it when it was plentiful and prices
were low so it could be distributed when prices were high, thus
providing a system of government price control. Like the Swiss
shelters, the structures were built according to specifications:
thus we find descriptions of them in the *Book of Odes*, beautiful
drawings in ancient scrolls, and stone engravings, all intended
to distribute ideas about the best design.[134] As Joseph Needham
writes, the structure "looks impregnable" with its frame of "heavy
timber, the roof of closely laid tiles, and the solid door—often
there are two—has double leaves and is fastened with a heavy
timber beam."[135] Beginning during the Han dynasty and continuing, unevenly, across two millennia come manuals of instructions
which, like the counting rules of CPR, give exact specifications
of the best way to build granaries. Treatises such as *Nung Cheng
Chhüan Shu* and *Shou Shih Thung Khao* specify even the "bricks
and tile to be used and the characters with which they were to
be stamped"; internal bays, each with its own door, measure 4.25

meters high by 3.5 meters wide by 5 meters deep; one bay is left empty so that the grain in each bay can be rotated to the next bay every six months, ensuring the grain will be "cooled and aired."[136] Needham's only sorrow is that none of the surviving manuals specify the exact design for the lanterns in the roof that ensure ventilation. Intended to equalize the availability of food across irregularities in the population and irregularities in the harvest, the "ever normal granary" (or "constantly normal granary" as it is first called in 54 BC)[137] is accompanied by systems to ensure "equable transport" in 115 BC and "equalization and standardization" of measure in 110 BC.[138]

Elaborate records from the Qing period show that the aspiration to ensure food for the population was carried out. In earlier dynasties, the principle is stated and there are references to the use of the granaries during famine, but the records are too fragmentary to be certain.[139] But by the Qing period (and especially 1644–1790, the very period during which Hobbes, Locke, and Rousseau were formulating the social contract theory that would underlie Western democracy) there is elaborate archival evidence. In the early eighteenth century, at least twelve Chinese provinces each store at least "one million bushels of grain." By the second half of the eighteenth century, year-by-year records exist for twenty provinces, showing stores in three types of granaries: the ever normal (state-run) granary, the community granaries, and the charity granaries.[140] As Pierre-Etienne Will and R. Bin Wong conclude, "The mid-Qing grain storage system was much more ambitious than any comparative storage program in Chinese history, not to mention that of other pre-modern civilizations."[141]

The country had three motives for guaranteeing the availabil-

ity of food: Confucian morality required nourishing the population for its own sake and taught that a population could only
aspire to virtue if survival were ensured; the governors needed
the support of the population for their expansionist plans; regular distribution of 30% of the grain prevented spoilage and
freshened the supplies.[142] These three motives could be fulfilled
only if the shelters themselves were made impregnable by design
and maintenance. As the Swiss shelters need to keep out radia-
tion, so the Chinese shelters had to keep out rain, fermentation,
and infestations by fungi, birds, insects, or rodents.[143] As the
Swiss system involves elaborate work beyond the physical con-
structions, so too the Qing attempt to ensure survival involved
elaborate record-keeping, documenting yearly rainfall, harvest
conditions, forms of ventilation, and storage amounts. Distribution itself was recognized as "an art," and alternative forms of
distribution were developed for lean, fertile, and normal production harvest.[144]

The millennium-long aspiration for equality of survival
makes all the more startling the spectacle of nuclear countries
that spend money on weapons and on shelters for those executive branch officers issuing the orders to fire the weapons, but
not on shelters for the population at large. As the United States
abandoned the project of shelters for its citizenry, so too did the
United Kingdom. Multiple documents show that prime ministers from Clement Attlee to Harold Wilson—the period from
1945 to 1970—concluded that it was impossible to protect the
population "at an affordable cost"; the damage, Attlee observes
in one document, would be of "a scale . . . against which any
civil defence preparations that were possible at the present time
would be ineffective."[145] If leaders perceive that a given form of

weaponry is so devastating that "no known protection" can be effective, should not those leaders begin to work frantically and relentlessly to eliminate such weapons from their own country and worldwide?

Instead, various British leaders procured the weapons, as well as an already existing shelter for themselves inside Box Hill in Wiltshire.[146] The recently declassified documents studied by historian Peter Hennessy reveal a 1963 War Cabinet compiling a list of who would be included in the 210-person Cotswold bunker, a list which omitted the Queen—the nuclear architects reasoned that she would be safer on the royal yacht, *Britannia*.[147] (Is a surface ship really a prudent place to be during a nuclear war?) A planning document entitled "Government War Book" was discreetly circulated in ninety-six copies during this same year, but not until two years later—two years after the Cuban Missile Crisis—did anyone notice that no copy had been sent to Buckingham Palace.[148] The Cotswold bunker was conceived of as a place, as the former head of the Ministry of Defence described it, "from which you could hope to restore some kind of government and make all kinds of arrangements from medical to food."[149] The documents Hennessy surveys, however, do not themselves show any preparatory thinking about "arrangements from medical to food"; and it is hard to picture how such arrangements could be initiated, let alone carried out, once an exchange of missiles had taken place. Did the War Cabinet imagine that though no shelters could protect against the bomb, somehow a surviving legion of nurses and cafeteria workers would be reachable by phone and able to start administering aid?

Far from working to ensure an equality of survival, the British executive officers at moments appear to have regarded the population's desire to survive as a detriment to the war effort. A report commissioned to describe the potential breakdown of government during nuclear war hypothesizes that "breakdown" occurs when

> the government of a country is no longer able to ensure that its orders are carried out. This state of affairs could come about through . . . the mass of people becoming preoccupied with their own survival rather than the country's war effort . . .[150]

Like the United States's repudiation of its citizenry, the disregard for the population of the United Kingdom helps us to contemplate the scale of achievement in the Swiss arrangements for a countrywide "vertical evacuation."

"Vertical evacuation" attempts to reestablish the right of exit, a right that has, for more than two thousand years, been recognized as essential to liberty. Some philosophers go further, asserting that it *is* liberty. The Stoic philosopher Epictetus (once himself a slave) accounts for freedom with the simple declaration, "I go where I please, I come whence I please."[151] Maurice Cranston, the biographer of Locke and translator of Rousseau, says that the Greek word for liberty, *eleutheria,* "in its etymology meant 'to go where one wills,'" and that the Latin word *libertas* is related to freedom of movement. Cranston argues that the right of exit is "the first and most fundamental of man's liberties."[152] Although other forms of freedom may have an equal claim to primacy, Cranston's description at the very least underscores the importance of the capacity to remove oneself from a situation to which one does not wish to be subject.

All the social contract theorists saw the human capacity to enter a political arrangement that was beneficial and to exit a political arrangement that was perilous as essential to consent theory, as is visible in the section of Hobbes's *Leviathan* entitled "A Review and Conclusion," again in Book Four, Chapter Two, of Rousseau's *Social Contract*, and in the famous Section 119 of Locke's *Second Treatise of Government* where he designates "tacit consent through residence" as the universal ground of consent. Although the inhabitants of countries practice their consent through many acts (such as forming constitutions, voting to ratify or reject a constitutional amendment, voting for an office holder, voting for a new law, running for office, acquiring citizenship), Locke argued that their willingness to reside inside a specific society which they were free to leave was the manifestation of their agreement to it, even if they had been born into a set of legal arrangements and had never voted for them.

Among other unspeakable harms, the weapons held by the eight nuclear states have eliminated the right of exit. With the exception of the Swiss underground, there is no space on earth that cannot be reached by the weapons. Many nations have worked to create nuclear-weapons-free zones that will increase the chance of survival and also create a sphere in which the right of exit is restored.[153] Those treaties—the 1996 Treaty of Pelindaba (Africa), the 1995 Treaty of Bangkok (South-East Asia), the 1968 Treaty of Tlatelolco (Mexico, Central, and South America), the 1985 Treaty of Rarotonga (South Pacific), the 1972 Seabed and Ocean Floor Treaty, the 1959 Antarctic Treaty—together cover a vast geographical spread. Crucially, they eliminate the possibility of possessing nuclear weapons from their own member states; the Treaty of Pelindaba, for example, which encompasses every country on the African continent as well as Madagascar, persuaded two countries with nuclear ambitions, South Africa and Algeria, to renounce those weapons.[154] In addition, such treaties encourage "habits of dialogue" among countries in any given region.[155] Each treaty serves as a model or precedent for the next (the language in Rarotonga is explicitly used in Pelindaba) and together they work to "delegitimize" nuclear weapons.[156] They may, in combination with many other avenues, eventually rid the earth of them.

But what the nuclear-weapons-free zones do not do, at present, is provide a shelter over the heads of the inhabitants or create a place of exit. Long-range US weapons can easily reach these populations. Nuclear weapons ships are not banned from entering nearby waters. In 2002, US President George Bush declined to sign the Bangkok Protocol, complaining that its provisions for protecting territorial waters limited US "freedom of navigation."[157] The only other nuclear-free-zone treaty that extends its protection to ocean waters is the Latin American Treaty of Tlatelolco; while it contains no blanket prohibition on the transit of ships carrying nuclear weapons, it gives member states individual discretion over whether such ships will be permitted to pass through their waters. The United States signed but stated that it rejected any aspect of the treaty compromising its "freedom at sea."[158] Over the last fifty years, "freedom of the seas" has repeatedly been invoked when any international constraint on the movement of submarines was proposed. When, as part of the 1971 Seabed Treaty, Yugoslavia stipulated that the United States contact a country whose coastal waters were about to be entered by a submarine, the United States strenuously objected.[159] When in 1985 New Zealand insisted that ships carrying nuclear weap-

ons stay out of their coastal waters and ports, the US
by disrupting the trilateral security treaty joining
States, Australia, and New Zealand.[160] The control
ties give their populations is limited. The Rarotonga Treaty, for
example, permits the US to test its delivery systems (though
not the weapons themselves) in the regional waters of the South
Pacific, and permits the US to station nuclear command and
control instruments on Australian ground.[161] In fact, none of
the treaties prohibit support facilities for some other country's
nuclear weapons on the soil of their member states.[162]

While, then, these treaties have accomplished critically important work, they do not make the populations living in the zones
immune to nuclear weapons. The Swiss shelter system aspires to
do exactly that. It is one of the few pieces of evidence we have
that the right of exit (as well as the "right to exist") is still imagin-
able in the nuclear age.

FOURTH MODEL:
THE CONSTITUTIONAL BRAKE ON WAR

The best "exit," the only "exit," from the obscene damage that
nuclear weapons are designed to bring about is the elimination
of the weapons themselves. That outcome is precisely what the
fourth model of emergency preparation would have brought
about had its procedures been practiced over the last sixty years.
That outcome can still be brought about—methodically and deci-
sively—if the United States population begins to follow those
procedures now. The two provisions in the US Constitution that
stipulate what must take place before we ever begin to injure a

foreign population are on every plane (logical, strategic, technical) profoundly incompatible with any form of weaponry that permits a president to authorize and enact the killings of tens of millions of people within several hours.

The question in an emergency, as we have repeatedly seen, is not *whether* habit structures will come into play but *which* habit structures will come into play. Our nuclear weapons, and the presidential first-use arrangements for their firing, are deep, elaborately practiced habits. Our fourteen Ohio-class submarines—each carrying the equivalent of 4,000 Hiroshima bombs—are moving across the ocean floor without cessation, day in and day out. The submarines come into their home ports in Kings Bay, Georgia, and Bangor, Washington, only long enough to shift crews; each submarine has two crews (one designated Gold, the other Blue), and each crew stays under the ocean for three months. During those ninety days—as Gerrit Oakes, an electronics technician on the USS *Maine*, reports—the all-male crew keeps "busy doing drills, training." Only on a single day out of the ninety days—"halfway through the patrol"—is there a special day and night "where we don't do any training."[163] As the secretary of the navy, Donald Winter, recently stated: "Although our nation has never fired a submarine-launched ballistic missile in anger, our Trident fleet [has the ability] to do so 24 hours a day, 7 days a week, 365 days a year."[164] Secretary Winter said this at a ceremony "commemorating the completion of 1,000 Trident strategic deterrent patrols"—that is, 3,000 months (or 250 years) of Ohio-class submarine patrols during which the fleet has maintained its instant nuclear-weapons-launch abilities. Like the submarines, the US land-based and air-based missiles stay in a constant state of practiced readiness.

The executive branch, too, stays in a state of readiness, with the briefcase containing the nuclear codes never more than one room away from the president. As the Natural Resources Defense Council points out: "The [strategic] war plans are not an outline of possibilities for the future *but a directive of what weapons must be put in place*: for key targets identified in the plan, *a warhead must be available and assigned to hit it at all times*."[165] The Natural Resources Defense Council also reports that during the George W. Bush administration, much work was undertaken to make the "preplanned strike options" more "adaptable" and "rapid," with an increased reliance on computerized computation.[166]

Standing against this lethal, genocide-ready arsenal are two provisions of the Constitution. While the United States does not at present have a civil defense system that protects its population, it does have a constitution that was designed to protect that population—and through that population, the people of other countries. The Constitution does not eliminate the possibility of war. But it does seek to ensure that war cannot be 1) entered into, and 2) sustained over a prolonged period, without reasons convincing enough to persuade large assemblies of people, both within the national legislature and within the population at large, of the need to injure foreign peoples.

Two crucial provisions—Article I, Section 8, Clause 11, and the Second Amendment—each ensure that there will be a distribution of military authority. One specifies that the power to declare war will be given to Congress, the full representative assembly. The option of giving this power to a smaller group—either the president acting alone or the Senate acting alone—was explicitly discussed and explicitly rejected at the constitutional convention. The power to declare war was given to the full assembly for three reasons: to ensure deliberation, to distribute authority, and to act as an emergency brake on the urge to go to war. The congressional obligation to oversee the nation's entry into war has been called the cornerstone of the Constitution by eighteenth- and nineteenth-century jurists. Justice Joseph Story, perhaps the country's greatest jurist, referred to it as "the highest act of legislation."

While the constitutional provision for a congressional declaration of war is a "law" consisting of a small number of words—"The Congress shall have power to declare war"—an elaborate protocol of steps is embedded in that clause, a protocol that includes the presentation in written form of what precisely is being declared; the guarantee of an equal voice to all members, majority or minority, that in turn ensures that if there is a counterargument to be made (most centrally, about whether a particular country does in fact deserve to be regarded as an "enemy"), it will be made; the explicit person-by-person polling and written recording of a vote by all 535 members; and the presentation to the US population—either during the event or in the hours immediately after—of a complete transcript of both the debate and the vote. Each of these, in turn, consists of a sequence of specified steps: the written form of the declaration must be read aloud three times so that all assembled understand what is at issue, and the speakers must proceed according to rules (such as the requirement that each speaker refer to other speakers by their office rather than their name) set out in advance in Thomas Jefferson's *A Manual of Parliamentary Practice* and by *Robert's Rules of Order*.

Congress was designated—along with the population as a whole—as the body responsible for overseeing our entry into war in part because Congress (in eras when it is functioning) practices the art of debating day in and day out. Imagine an assembly that only waited until it was on the threshold of war to decide what rules of speaking it would follow, what forms of verbal opposition it would hold to be fair and unfair, how the array of speakers would be sequenced, what rules of evidence it would accept. It could be said that all congressional deliberation during peacetime, no matter how trivial or grand the subject, is a rehearsal, a constant act of practicing, for the moment when it will be called upon to debate the gravest matter of all, the matter of going to war.

The same logic underwrites the Second Amendment. A population that bears the responsibility for questions about going to war becomes a population capable of high level of debate; conversely, a population that forfeits that responsibility allows its powers of deliberation to deteriorate.[167] Just as Article I, Section 8, Clause 11, distributes the declaratory power to the full assembly, so the Second Amendment distributes authority to the whole enfranchised population. It rejects the notion of "a standing army," a fixed army subject to executive control and cut off from civilian life (as is closely approximated today due to the replacement of draft by a recruited army). It insists instead on a "militia" or "citizen's army," an army drawn from the full population uniformly across geography and across wealth. According to the record of the ratification debates at the time the Constitution was circulating to the states, without a proper distribution of arms, an executive army presents as much threat to the social contract as does a foreign army, since in both cases the population is "invaded," "disarmed," and infantilized back into a state of pre-contractual coercion.

The Second Amendment does not stipulate how much injuring power the country will have; it may have very little or a great
deal. It stipulates, instead, that however much the country has,
the authority for its use must be equally distributed across the
population. This principle of equal distribution has been saluted
in other countries by militarists and pacifists alike. For example,
in the first General Assembly in France in 1789, Mirabeau said
that the aristocracy had been created merely by endowing one
group of citizens with arms and depriving the other group of
arms. Similarly, Gandhi said that of the eleven evil acts committed by the British against India, the worst was the disarming of
the population ("Give us back our arms," he said, "and then we'll
tell you whether or not we're going to use them").

Congress and the population in concert act as a double brake
on the executive urge to identify another population as an enemy.
Legal rules are meant to be internalized into a set of practices
that automatically go into effect: when a crisis arises, Congress
begins to deliberate and the population begins to debate. But
since the invention of nuclear weapons, there has been no congressional declaration even for the conventional wars in Korea,
Vietnam, the Gulf, the former Yugoslavia, Iraq, or the invasions
of Panama and Haiti.[168] Following Vietnam, the disappearance
of the draft eliminated the distribution of military responsibility
across the population, eliminating as well the exercise of popular debate and dissent. Because in the present era these constitutional provisions have lapsed, when a crisis arises Congress
and the population wait passively for an announcement from the
president and the joint chiefs of staff about what "the country"
will do.

Although the fourth model of emergency preparation has

focused on one constitution in particular, that of the United States, other countries have constitutional provisions that may (along with international law) eventually enable their populations to eliminate their nuclear arsenals. For example, Article 35 of the French constitution stipulates that "A declaration of war must be authorized by Parliament." Article 34, Clause 4, confers on Parliament the obligation to "determine the fundamental principles of the general organization of national defense." The present arrangements in France—a presidential first-use policy, the inclusion of fewer than twenty people in the formation of nuclear policy,[169] and the issuing of executive edicts that sweep aside legislative authority[170]—all violate the constitution and would themselves be eliminated if the constitution were applied.

In India, Article 246, Clause 1, of the constitution stipulates the "Subject Matter" for which Parliament is responsible: "Defense of India and every part thereof including preparation for defence and all such acts as may be conducive in time of war to its prosecution and after its termination to effective demobilization." Subsequent items for which the legislature is responsible include all forms of military force.[171]

The 1993 constitution of the Russian Federation is widely perceived as conferring vast power on the country's president, but some of its structural features resemble those found in the Constitution of the United States. If Russia is attacked—if its borders are violated by armed aggression—the president may begin to act at once to defend the country (Article 87) and then notify the legislature. But while the president may take unilateral action to defend the interior of the country, Article 102 stipulates that the use of military force outside the borders requires the authorization of the Federal Council (the analogue of the US Senate), and Article 106 assigns to the Federal Council the responsibility for protecting the borders and overseeing war and peace. Legislative debate, deliberation, and testing of the proposition that a foreign population deserves to be injured therefore appear to be key parts of the structure of governance. Russia also has a constitutional provision that resembles the Second Amendment of the US Constitution: Article 59 distributes to the entire population shared responsibility for defending the country. The only way to make nuclear weapons compatible with these three constitutional requirements is to eliminate those weapons altogether.

Not all eight of the nuclear states have explicit constitutional provisions that make the legislature or the population a brake on the urge to go to war. But countries which lack such provisions have in recent years sometimes voiced the need to acquire one. In the United Kingdom, for example, proposals to require a parliamentary declaration of war prior to taking British troops into battle have been introduced at regular intervals in the first decade of the twenty-first century.[172] In Pakistan, although the constitution has no provision stipulating which branch of the government declares war, the April 2010 passage of the Eighteenth Amendment strengthened the legislative and judicial branches and diminished the power of the presidency.[173]

Is it the case that a population's consent is entailed in the fighting of war? It is often said that soldiers follow orders, but it is hard to find a war, from the Trojan War to Vietnam, that is independent of the deliberations of its military men and women. Soldiers' strikes, acts of desertion, and disobedience, for example, played a stunning role in the 1989–90 revolutions in Europe. The East German army, once renowned for its discipline and

training, was drastically reduced by desertions w'
between November and March. Its size fell by almo
173,000 to 90,000; remaining soldiers sometimes ∈
reluctance to participate in ordinary activities such as the
tary exercises carried out by Soviet troops.[174] In late Decembe.
Romanian soldiers took the side of the population they had
been ordered to suppress and in doing so brought about the
fall of Ceauşescu. At the end of March, after the Soviet army in
Lithuania had received "permission to use violence" against the
population, almost 2,000 Lithuanian soldiers deserted, formally
registering their names at the parliament building in Vilnius.[175]
Vietnam, World War I, the American Civil War, and scores of
others provide rich evidence of the fact that wars are only fought
with the soldiers' consent.

Complaints are often made that involving Congress and the
population in war decisions will slow down the act of going to
war because so much energy is needed to persuade them. That
is precisely what the Constitution intended. Here we encoun-
ter a key attribute differentiating our first three models of emergency preparation—CPR, voluntary associations, and the Swiss
shelter system—and the constitutional provisions for overseeing
our entry into war.

Rather than specifying the taking of an action, the Constitution instead requires that we stop and deliberate about whether
to take an action. This difference arises because of a starker difference. In those emergencies where the diminution of injury is
at stake, all deliberative habits are directed toward determining
how to minimize the injury, not to the question of *whether* we
ought to minimize the injury. If a fire has broken out in a grain
elevator, we do not wonder whether to put it out but how to

put it out in the most efficient and damage-minimizing way. If a swimmer has stopped breathing, no one deliberates whether we ought to help him start breathing, but only the sequence of acts that will bring his breath back.

There exist highly anomalous situations where we do debate whether to continue administering aid, such as extended care for tiny premature infants or for injured persons on full life support. But these perplexing problems warrant a great deal of our attention precisely because they are so at odds with the ordinary imperative to give aid. Furthermore, the very reason they occasion deliberation is because a grave question has arisen about whether the aid that is being administered diminishes the injury or instead perpetuates or even amplifies it. Far from contradicting the norm, then, these apparently anomalous cases instead confirm it: deliberation is directed to how, not whether, to diminish the injury.[176]

Precisely the opposite is the case where the action to be performed is not the diminution of injury, but its infliction. The social contract exists in order to prohibit injury. In its purest form—were a pure form possible—no injury would ever be legal. In its ideal form, the social contract has as its first and fundamental law a never-injure rule; even in reality, it comes close to having a never-injure rule. But there are—as both Thomas Hobbes and John Locke make explicit—two *and only two* situations in which the absolute prohibition on injuring is lifted: the punishment of criminals and going to war.[177] Both of these situations are ones in which the wrongdoers—the criminals, the enemy population—have acquired the status of wrongdoer precisely by having broken the never-injure rule and so must themselves be stopped, even if stopping them requires injuring

them. But because the members of the social contrac[t]
inflicting injury on the criminal or on the enemy, be
ing an action that is deeply at odds with the first ru[le]
social contract, their act of injuring can be done only after going
through exhausting procedural gates (e.g., jury trial, congressional declaration of war, the deliberation by the population)
designed to test whether it is really the case that the alleged
wrongdoers have in fact broken the never-injure rule.[178] Only if
the allegation of wrongdoing can withstand the sustained scrutiny of twelve people in the case of criminal wrongdoing and
535 people in the case of the congressional declaration, will the
never-injure prohibition be lifted and the criminal punished or
the enemy attacked. Only if hundreds of thousands of citizens
ratify that congressional decision by agreeing that the country
designated "enemy" needs to be stopped will the war (declared
by Congress) ever become materialized reality.[179]

• • •

The overarching framework that emerges into view has three
alternative outcomes. What occurs in an emergency is either
immobilization (Artaud's theatregoer; Arendt's Eichmann; the
unconscious ambulance patient), or incoherent action (Aesop's
donkey failing to distinguish salt and sponges), or coherent
action (CPR, the Canadian social contracts, the Swiss shelter
system, the US constitutional provisions overseeing war). Those
are the three alternatives. Clearly immobilization and incoherent
action are not outcomes to emulate. What needs to be undertaken, then, is an assessment of a coherent action, and almost
all instances of coherent emergency action entail high degrees
of habit.

The question is not: Do emergency and habit go together?

They do go together. If we can act, we do so out of the habitual. Habit yokes thought and action together. If no serviceable habit is available, we will use an unserviceable one and become either immobilized or incoherent. Instead the question is: To what extent are the habitual and the deliberative compatible? Behind the question of the habitual is the question of laws, since habit is an internalizing regulating mechanism that has its external equivalent in law; the bond is manifest in the nearby term "custom," used in everyday speech as a synonym both for habit and for law. Insofar as I am making an argument about finding and following good habits, I am also making an argument about finding and following, binding ourselves to, good constitutional procedures. Conversely, I am suggesting that our contempt for our laws, the suspension of constitutional requirements overseeing our entry into war, is in part based on our contempt for the habitual that is undeserved.

Chapter Three

THE PLACE OF HABIT
IN ACTS OF THINKING

The rejection of procedures and constitutional guarantees, this book has so far suggested, comes from three sources: first, the belief that action requires putting aside thinking; second, the belief that action does in fact normally require thinking but that *rapid* action requires putting aside thinking; and third, the belief that thinking requires setting aside habit. In the first two, thinking is rejected in the name of action. In the third, habit is set aside in the name of thinking. This third error is as grave as the first two. We have seen that habit is everywhere visible in effective emergency preparation. In turn, thinking—as the section below will show—is profoundly visible in the lineaments of habit.

It is not hard to see why the kind of deliberative act connected to an emergency has some features that make it hard to recognize as an act of deliberation. Deliberation normally inhabits a temporal space close to the action which is its outcome. If one deliberates about the best book to read, that is usually followed by reaching for the book. If one chooses the best horse to ride, that is usually followed by mounting the horse. The same is true

of group decisions; a faculty that debates a rule change will usually take a vote and institute the decision soon after the deliberations. But in the case of emergency procedures, there is apt to be
a long temporal break between the deliberation and the actual
enactment, which must wait for the emergency. There is a long
pause between figuring out CPR procedures and the moment
one is called upon to use that knowledge. There is a long pause
between designing and building the shelter system of Switzerland and the moment of its use. There is a long pause between
the debates on the best constitutional procedures to protect a
country on the threshold of war and the moment forty, or one
hundred, or two hundred years later when the crucial test of the
braking power of these procedures comes.

The mystification that is caused by the distance between the
deliberation and the action is compounded by a second problem. Not only must the procedure be made habitual, but it must
be inscribed as habit in the most highly self-conscious way. In
ordinary life, the more useful a habit is the stronger it will grow,
simply because each day will provide the occasion to practice it.
There is no need to set aside a few days a year to practice reading or driving a car; life keeps putting in front of us daily problems that occasion the practice of those actions. But emergencies
do not occur often, and therefore there is no naturally arising
occasion on which the appropriate procedure can be practiced.
The habit must instead be acquired by a highly willed act of
internalization and may seem to be an artificial exercise without
an object. Emergency procedures may come to seem the empty
offspring of the space of waiting and the place of drill.

Our everyday estimate of habit unreflectingly places it outside
thought, outside human will, outside ethics. But a rich philo-

sophic tradition—classical Greek and Christian writers,[1] Anglo-American thinkers,[2] and continental theorists[3]—has seen habit as a powerful tool of cognition. It is the relation between habit and one specific form of thinking, deliberation, that most directly illuminates the way we think in an emergency, since deliberation is thinking directed toward the taking of an action. But the place of habit in deliberation will itself be clearer if it is preceded by a consideration of two other mental events, sensory perception and creation—mental events that are themselves elaborately in play in an emergency.

HABIT AND SENSATION

Habit is never seen as something that makes a slight adjustment in the character of sensory perception, dulling perception (if one judges habit to be a negative) or enhancing it (if one judges it as positive). It is instead understood to cut to the heart of sensation, either closing it down entirely or instead building up perception at its own interior and even bringing it into being. If these two views are taken together, they do not balance one another or cancel one another out. Remarkably, they together work to validate the positive view. They together show that habit is an immensely powerful agent for regulating, even creating, the acuity of sentience. Just as one may regulate the amount of light by opening and closing one's eyelids or by turning and tilting one's head through hundreds of angles and planes, so habit acts to set in place countless gateways that either open and allow the world to rush toward one or instead close it to keep it wholly at bay. The way the negative and positive account together validate the positive account will be clearer if we for a moment contemplate the two views in isolation from one another.

The negative account sees habit as incompatible with sensory acuity and, ultimately, with sensation itself. Habit makes us—in some almost literal way—insensate, insensible. Montaigne articulates this view. He takes smell as his model instance. How quickly we grow used to the presence of an odor, and when we grow used to it, it at once disappears: "Habit stupefies our senses. . . . My perfumed doublet is pleasant to my nose, but after I have worn it three days in a row it is pleasant only to the noses of others."[4] Any sensation which is enduring, repetitive, or perpetual may similarly become lost to us. The extraordinary adaptability of the sense of smell, rather than being taken as "exceptional," becomes for Montaigne paradigmatic of all the senses. What is true of smell is true of hearing, as he illustrates with a story about his gradually acquired ability to sleep through troublesome church bells. But we sleep not only through church bells; we even sleep through the music of the spheres, the "marvelous harmony" produced by the solid bodies of the spheres "coming to touch and rub on one another as they roll." Thick and leaden with habituation, we become insensible to the perpetual sound of the cosmos, a deprivation which in turn works to deepen our leadenness. Church bells and the music of the spheres are not randomly chosen: the habitual closes us out from things of great beauty and spirit.

The concreteness of Montaigne is important. When he complains that habit makes us insensible, he is not simply using a loosely pejorative word; he means very literally that sensory perception is incapacitated, "stupefied," "put to sleep." This conception of habit is today presented as a general complaint about the way it disposes us to be "insensitive," "robotic," "automatic," or "inanimate." Samuel Beckett called habit "a great deadener" (despite the fact that throughout his plays, lifesaving rules of survival always entail elaborate repertoires of habit).[5] The very vividness of these words, and the unmarked modulation from "insensitive" to "insensate" to "inanimate," might make us lose sight of the literalness of the claim that lies behind each.

Aliveness is often perceived to be at issue, not only by the great detractors of habit but by its champions. Both Aristotle and William James, for example, give celebratory accounts of habit, and both enlist the issue of aliveness centrally into those accounts. For Aristotle it is precisely the acquisition of habit that marks the fact of our being animate, differentiates us from the inanimate. Stones falling and fires rising, though they might day after day repeat these actions, do not do them from habit, because they are incapable of willing the acquisition of that behavior. Far from cutting us off from the music of the spheres, it is exactly the work of habit, says Aristotle, to bring the highest things within our reach, even if they appear to arrive by some path beyond our own agency. In the *Nicomachean Ethics*, he questions whether the greatest excellences, and the happiness that attends them, come from the gods or instead from "learning or by habituation or . . . training." He concludes that though "godlike," they are often not "god-sent" but acquired by "some process of learning or training."[6]

William James shares Aristotle's regard for the enabling power of habit, but he does not see it as the feature which separates the inanimate and animate worlds. Repeated actions performed by inanimate objects and repeated actions undertaken by animate creatures look similar to him because he attends to the acquisition of habits of perception as they take place in the brain and spinal cord—that is, as they inscribe themselves into the material substance of the human being. The suppleness of sensation we acquire through habituation is continuous with the suppleness acquired by material objects: a dress folds more easily once a crease is set; a river runs in the banks it established in the last storm; a key turns in the lock with more ease on its three-hundredth turn than on its first turn; a violin absorbs into its interior a way of handling consistent with the musician's level of skill;[7] and the quality of the instrument's musical habituation partially determines its value to the next buyer. Like the body of the violin, the tissue of the brain can acquire varying levels of sensory acuity.

James pictures the formation of habits of perception as they occur at the neuronal level. The key word linked to "habit" is "plasticity," which he defines as structures "weak enough to yield to an influence, but strong enough not to yield all at once." It is this feature, above all others, that he attributes to our brains:

> Organic matter, especially nervous tissue, seems endowed with a very extraordinary degree of plasticity of this sort; so that we may without hesitation lay down as our first proposition the following, that *the phenomena of habit in living beings are due to the plasticity of the organic materials of which their bodies are composed.*[8]

The brain and spinal cord are the extreme examples of habits, which are "due to the plasticity of materials to outward agents." They are encased in "bony boxes" so that they will not be responsive to mechanical or thermal pressure, yet will be highly responsive to sensory nerve influences.[9] In choosing the material artifacts of dress, key, and violin as analogues for sensation, James acknowledges the artifactual, self-constructed character of sensation. It is not something that happens to us but something whose happening we shape and direct, just as we willfully inscribe into the dress, key, or violin the paths of future folds, turns, and resonances.

Our brain is our primary instrument. Like the violin whose "fibers of . . . wood contract habits of vibration" from the master it belongs to,[10] so the matter of the brain contracts habits of alertness from the master it belongs to. Any theorist who holds that sensory acuity is achieved by habit will also be a theorist committed to education. So James writes, "Could the young but realize how soon they will become mere walking bundles of habits, they would give more heed to their conduct while in the plastic state. We are spinning our own fates . . . Every smallest stroke of virtue or of vice leaves its never so little scar."[11] Aristotle's formulation is even stronger: "It makes no small difference then, whether we form habits of one kind or another from our youth; it makes a very great difference, or rather all the difference."[12]

Precisely this constellation of claims about habit—its connection to sensation, to the highest spiritual accomplishments, and to education—is central to John Dewey, whose positive account of sensory perception is, to a degree not shared by Aristotle or James, as concrete as Montaigne's negative account. Even to be able to pick out of the world a specifiable odor such as the perfume of Montaigne's doublet, or to sort out the sound of the church bell from a welter of other sensory sensations (such as the feel of the bed on which Montaigne is tossing and turning) is a labor; in the time prior to actually hearing the church bell, we have, according to Dewey, constructed our own ability to do so.

Dewey's example is not sound or odor but color:

> [D]istinct and independent sensory qualities, far from being original elements, are the products of a highly skilled analysis which disposes of immense technical scientific resources. To be able to single out a definitive sensory element in any field is evidence of a high degree of previous training, that is, of well-formed habits. A moderate amount of observation of a child will suffice to reveal that even such gross discriminations as black, white, red, green, are the result of some years of active dealings with things in the course of which habits have been set up. It is not such a simple matter to have a clear-cut sensation. The latter is a sign of training, skill, habit."[13]

If, as Dewey argues, it takes "some years of active dealing with things" to reliably discriminate green, blue, or red, how many years of practice are required to reach the adult state in which the average human being is capable of distinguishing 26,000 colors, or over 2.3 million if "gray value" (or lightness) is included?[14] In turn, what ardor and practice are required to move beyond these "average" capacities to become an exquisite colorist like the Venetians (with their habits of optical mixing), or like Matisse (whose paintings induce retinal arabesques), or like the virtuoso landscape gardeners Gertrude Jekyll or Claude Monet?

This question begins to carry us to the realm of artists and inventors, to which we will soon turn in the section on the place of habit in the mental act of creation. But the nature of sensation should remain in front of us for a bit longer. In addition to habits of sensation, Dewey frequently speaks of habits of acute observation and inference,[15] habits of thought and active inquiry.[16] But the acuity of sensory perception remains key. It allows us "to respond freshly and generously to each incident in life."[17]

The negative and the positive accounts, so strikingly at odds, eventually reinforce one another. For Montaigne, we start with a sensation and habit acts to dampen it down, threatening to subtract it all together from the perceivable surface of the world. For Dewey, there is no sensation to begin with, only a welter of confused and scrambled signals; eventually the active and labor-intensive effort of attention enables us to distinguish a discrete sensory event. For Montaigne, habit puts aliveness in peril by making sensory perception closer to sleep than to waking. For Dewey, habit heightens the felt experience of aliveness and by steadily heightening our perceptual acuity greatly contributes to our ability to keep ourselves alive. The two views not only coexist, but coexist within any one writer. The very great tribute Montaigne eventually bestows on habit will be encountered in a later section of this chapter; and Dewey periodically interrupts his celebratory account to voice complaints about the negative outcomes of habit.[18]

The fact that habit is held responsible for both insensitivity and supersensitivity works to credit the positive place of habit in sensory cognition. Perhaps this double capacity requires no elaboration: everyone recognizes that repeated exposure to per-fumes may make one nose-blind to their smell or may instead enable one to grow exquisitely adept at distinguishing a warm rose and wood scent from one that combines jasmine and violet greens.

The neurological basis of this two-directional plasticity has been worked out with extraordinary clarity is one particular realm of sensory perception, not color or odor or sound or taste but that of touch, specifically physical pain. The revolutionary but widely accepted "gate control theory of pain"—developed by neuroscientist Ronald Melzack and biologist Patrick Wall—rejects the Cartesian picture of an external pain stimulus acting on the surface of the body and ringing a bell cord that proceeds in a linear fashion to the brain. It posits instead a gate on the spinal cord where—even before we begin to feel the pain or identify the part of the body where it is taking place—cultural habits, familial habits, and individual habits are brought to bear on the apprehension of the pain, either closing down the gate so that we do not feel the sensation as acutely as the stimulus itself would warrant or opening the gate more widely so that its aversive affects are felt in full force.[19] The complex neurobiology at work in the brain's gate control structure may one day help us come to understand the neural structures that clarify the way habit and learning work in wholly pain-free forms of sensory perception, whether seeing color or hearing a bird's song. It will help to explain why learning, and self-directed habits of attention, can vastly magnify our sensory powers.

HABIT AND MENTAL CREATION

As in the realm of sensation, so in the realm of creation we find both a damning and a celebratory account of habit. Familiar to most people is the view that artistic improvisation and engineering inventiveness exist at one end of a spectrum that has at its opposite pole the phenomenon of habit. The poet, the dancer, the composer, the painter, the inventor seem at some far remove from the realm of habit. Yet equally familiar to most people is the key part played by habit in achieving and maintaining creative virtuosity: the labor-intensive daily drill ballet dancers undergo, the five-hours-a-day-every-day practice of violinists. Gershwin first learned his instrument as a child when he went to play at the home of a friend whose family had an automatic player piano (an instrument he first saw in the penny arcade at the age of six); he placed his hands on the moving keys and eventually found that when he carried his hands to a piano that was not automated, he could reproduce the same virtuosity.[20]

The richness and depth of the two opposing views can be efficiently apprehended by concentrating on one person of great inventive genius, Benjamin Franklin, and the ways in which he is described by two people, both themselves hugely influential artists, one of whom is dazzled by Franklin and the other of whom scorns him. The positive account is provided by the American architect and architectural theorist Robert Venturi, who has reconstructed Franklin's house in Philadelphia and attached to it a celebratory museum. The negative account is provided by the British poet and novelist D. H. Lawrence.

Benjamin Franklin provides a good case for three reasons. First, he is a great inventor: bifocals, grocer's stick, swimming fins, a university, reading clubs, street lights, and international treaties are among the things he invented or helped to create. Second, his inventions were often occasioned by what he saw as a latent emergency; the moment he mentions the dangers posed by the dark streets of Philadelphia, one can see in his prose his nostrils begin to dilate and the nerves in his face begin to flicker like a wild animal who has just caught a scent. The scent is invention. Throughout Franklin's autobiography and letters, his recognition of a problem occasions an adrenaline rush of invention. Third, his idea of invention is directly yoked to habit. Franklin believes that in order to make a creditable invention one must first make the object, and then make certain that the instructions for making it are legible enough that so that everyone else can make it too. A pair of bifocals or a glass harmonica only becomes a successful creation once it is distributable, habitual.

This principle applies to what Franklin regarded as one of his greatest inventions: himself. His autobiography is a set of instructions on how to make a Benjamin Franklin—how, in effect to make a great inventor, or whatever that person is who throughout the book stands in front of us. This desire to make the conditions of his own construction legible in turn occasions his inclusion of the charts of vices and virtues that enabled him deliberately to shape needed habits. Inventors who lived after Franklin have sometimes taken his instructions to heart. Tolstoy's early diaries have lists to regulate what he will do at the gaming table, lists for what he will say in the drawing room, lists for how he will inscribe a new prose style into himself, and these lists are punctuated with open acknowledgments that his teacher is Benjamin Franklin.[21] But Tolstoy's admiration is encoded in his own imitation of Franklin rather than in an extended set of descriptions, and so for the negative and positive views it is illuminating to turn to Lawrence and Venturi.

The views of Franklin held by Lawrence and Venturi constitute a conversation not just about one particular inventor but about a style of invention that eventually radiates throughout the United States, for Franklin is regarded by both artists as helping to form the spirit of America. Lawrence writes, "I just utter a long loud curse against Benjamin and the American corral." In fact, not just this sentence but the whole essay is one "long loud curse" against Franklin and his country. Surely this essay holds the record for sustaining the mode of the exclamatory, even for the sheer number of exclamation marks. "The Perfectibility of Man! Ah heaven, what a dreary theme! The perfectibility of the Ford car!" Though Lawrence distributes his scorn widely over Franklin's attributes, his charts of virtues and vices come in for special scorn: "the first of Americans practised this enticing list with assiduity"; he "gave himself good marks and bad marks"; he gave his countrymen "conduct charts" and "virtues in columns." Lawrence's ten-page curse against Franklin's American ethic contains, like all curses, the wish for its destruction. It ends, "Now is your chance, Europe. Now let Hell loose and get your own back . . . Let Hell loose, and get your own back, Europe!"[22]

Venturi's architectural portrait of Benjamin Franklin—his reconstruction of Franklin's house and the museum (or hall of fun) that adjoins it—dedicates itself to the attributes of capaciousness and vivacity. One section of the museum contains a closet whose silver interior is covered with mirrors on all four walls; on the mirrors in flashing neon script are the words "Inventor," "Statesman," "Printer," "Revolutionary," "Treaty Maker" all pulsing in bright colors. As one stands inside the closet, the endlessly reflected waves of script seem to be moving toward and away from one in all directions, so that one experiences what it must have been like to be inside the pulsing consciousness of Benjamin Franklin, his hot pink inventorliness passing through his bright green statesmanship and nearly colliding with the blue of his revolutionary dimension which in turn has braided to his treaty-making. One senses his largeness and largesse.

Lawrence's portrait is precisely the opposite. Not capaciousness but a closing down is what he stresses. Though Franklin receives many adjectives from Lawrence, the main ones are little-ness and the absence of color. "He was a little model, was Benjamin. Doctor Franklin. Snuff-coloured little man!" And again, "Middle-sized, sturdy, snuff-coloured Doctor Franklin, one of the soundest citizens." "There is a certain earnest naïveté about him. Like a child. And like a little old man." And again, "I'm not going to be turned into a virtuous little automaton as Benjamin would have me. 'This is good, this is bad. Turn the little handle and let the good tap flow,' saith Benjamin, and all America with him." Eventually Lawrence asks, "And why, oh why should the snuff-coloured little trap have wanted to take us all in?" On the final page, Franklin is still in Philadelphia "setting up this unlovely, snuff-coloured little ideal, or automaton, of a pattern American."[23]

Venturi pictures the interior of Franklin in throbbing Technicolor; Lawrence pictures him as snuff-colored and miniaturized. Oddly, it is not that Lawrence fails to see how many actions Franklin performed: he includes a Franklinesque list—that he "lighted the streets of young Philadelphia . . . invented electrical appliances . . . was a member of all the important councils of Philadelphia . . . won the cause of American Independence at the French Court, and was the economic father of the United States." Lawrence even pictures Franklin as single-handedly overthrowing Europe: "He wanted the whole European apple-cart upset"; he made "a small but very dangerous hole in the side of England, through which hole Europe has by now almost bled to death."[24] Yet precisely the teeming layering of persons in Venturi's mirrors are what Lawrence claims are shut down by Franklin—he asserts that he, Lawrence, is many men and Franklin wants him to choose and be only one. Lawrence, however large, seems homogeneous when standing by the side of the heterogeneous Benjamin Franklin, who seems to be carrying a small crowd of persons around inside of him.

The other image Lawrence uses as persistently as "small" and "snuff-colored" is the barbed wire fence. "This is Benjamin's barbed wire fence. He made himself a list of virtues, which he trotted inside like a grey nag in a paddock." "Here am I now in tatters and scratched to ribbons, sitting in the middle of Benjamin's America looking at the barbed wire . . . the American corral." "Benjamin tries to shove me into a barbed wire paddock." "America . . . Absolutely got down by her own barbed wire of shalt-nots."[25] The view is once again in precise opposition to Venturi's. Reconstructing Benjamin Franklin's house, Venturi leaves the walls entirely un-filled in; he gives us only the outline of the house, etched in steel, like an elegant architectural pencil sketch. Far from being constricting, the house is airy, open to the sky and the sounds of the street. The domestic habits of self-construction, despised by Lawrence, are venerated by Venturi: he inscribes into the floor passages from Benjamin's letters from France to his wife, listing the blue material for house curtains, consulting with her whether the material is appropriate for the hangings. The phantom blue curtains are as airy as the sky. The fleeting sound of a voice making its way across the Atlantic is Venturi's salute to Franklin's charts, lists, and daily letters of domestic self-invention.

This split between the constricting and the expansive seems perhaps the most mysterious opposition. Other oppositions in the views of Venturi and Lawrence are value-laden, and it is therefore understandable that their assessments might diverge.

But this one, because it is sheerly descriptive, seems as though it should acquire more stability. The division stands for a large split, for the two reactions are applicable to many contexts where invention and procedure are coupled. Is the Swiss shelter system Venturi's image of throbbing Technicolor ingenuity? To me it is: I believe the Swiss and their procedures for protecting their population and their special objects will survive anything. Or is it instead the case, as many people believe, that Switzerland is correctly described as snuff-colored, small, full of barbed-wire regulations? Should we give a standing ovation to the residents of the Saskatchewan plains for their lists specifying what equipment each person must bring to a fire, or should those lists be dismissed as "virtue in columns"? Is learning CPR a boring act of self-miniaturization or is it closer to a glass harmonica in its otherworldly virtuosity?[26]

Above all, are the laws specifying the gates the people of the United States are obligated to pass through before they injure a foreign population—Article I, Section 8, Clause 11, and the Second Amendment—snuff-colored procedural regulations that we can shrug off with impunity as we have tried to do for the last six decades, or are they vibrant inventive genius writ large, the palladial alphabet of a country that aspires to be a great and a good democracy? When the citizens of Athens were scheduled to meet in assembly, a flag was raised above the city at daybreak so that the city's 30,000 citizens would remember to come. Those who arrived late were marked with paint and fined for their tardiness.[27] In the United States, neither the congressional assembly nor the citizens convene as the issue of going to war is debated in private conversations behind closed doors at the White House.

Before he was a presidential candidate, Senator Barack Obama spoke at the John F. Kennedy Library about the painful discrepancy between the Illinois state legislature, where attendance by all members is required during deliberations, and the US Congress, where during most debates the hall is empty, with a few staffers milling in and out.[28] As President George W. Bush prepared to invade Iraq in February 2003, Senator Robert C. Byrd stood on the floor of the Senate and denounced its muteness:

> [T]his nation stands at the brink of battle . . . [Y]et this Chamber is for the most part ominously, dreadfully silent. . . . There is no debate. There is no discussion. There is no attempt to lay out for the Nation the pros and cons of this particular war. There is nothing.

Silent, despite the fact that—as Byrd went on to say—the United States was about to launch "a massive unprovoked military attack on a nation which is over 50% children." Silent, despite the fact that the executive branch was about to introduce a dangerous new doctrine of preemption, attacking not a country that was a present threat but a country that might someday in the future become one. Silent, despite the fact that the executive "recently refused to take nuclear weapons off the table when discussing a possible attack against Iraq."[29]

If we should someday have a president who recognizes that he or she cannot legally go to war without first going to Congress and asking for a declaration, would Congress even remember how to carry out such deliberations? Equally important, would the United States population recognize the importance of restoring this constitutional provision? Four days before he was elected president, Bill Clinton said in an interview that he would never take this country to war without a congressional declaration,[30] a statement that might have prompted people to dance in the streets. But there was no confetti; the streets remained quiet, and even the interviewer appeared not to have noticed what the candidate had just said and simply changed the subject. Once he was elected, President Clinton invaded Haiti and the former Yugoslavia on his own authority, oiling the machinery of illegal executive habits that would make it easier for the next president to roll into Iraq, killing more than 100,000 civilians—and reinforcing the long-standing nuclear arrangements for presidential first-use.

HABIT AND DELIBERATION

Are there—as there were in the spheres of sensory perception and creation—both negative and positive accounts of the place of habit in mental deliberation? Certainly both accounts are audible in the concrete instance of the deliberation required for a congressional declaration of war. On the one hand, it is perceived as the greatest and gravest safeguard of the social contract because it specifies that we can only be released from the never-injure rule by going through a deliberately encumbering set of steps before lifting the prohibition. It was for this reason that Justice Story called Article I, Section 8, Clause 11 the "highest act of legislation" and suggested that far from being too encumbering, it would be reasonable to add "greater restrictions" to it.[31] On the other hand, the requirement for a congressional declaration has been (and continues to be) denigrated by many people in the twentieth and twenty-first centuries as a set of baffling and unnecessary impediments to the taking of an urgent national action.

The more general theoretical question about deliberation and habit, however, is less likely to be openly debated than the relation of sensory perception and habit or creation and habit, because detractors of habit, believing that it shuts down sensation and that it exists at an opposite pole from creation, are not likely even to get to the question of its relation to deliberation. But what is striking is the fact that deliberation and habit share key attributes, and their relation can be approached by looking at the overlapping accounts of these attributes. Crucially, the role of material obstruction (which we regularly associate with habit) turns out to be assigned a key role in the philosophic accounts of deliberation: the focus on impedimenta in debates about the congressional declaration of war, for example, is consistent with a broader perception of the place of impedimenta in deliberation of any kind. Conversely, governance (which we regularly associate with deliberation) turns out to be assigned a key role in the philosophic accounts of habit. It will be helpful to begin with the second, before turning back to the first.

Deliberation and Governance / Habit and Governance

Deliberation and governance are so inextricably linked that—as we saw at the opening of this book—political philosophers who have written treatises on the one tend also to have written treatises on the other: Plato, Aristotle, Locke, Hobbes, Hume, and Mill convince us that the two subjects occupy shared ground.

Ideas govern the state because, as Locke writes in *Conduct of the Understanding*, they govern our individual actions: "in truth the ideas and images in men's minds are the invisible powers that constantly govern them, and to these they all universally pay a ready submission."[32] It is precisely because the understanding exercises this governing power that the "conduct of the understanding" is so important. As good ideas make possible good governance, so bad ideas that take over the mind are described by Locke in images of illegal governance: "matters" can "take possession of our minds with a kind of authority and will not be kept out or dislodged, but, as if the passion that rules were for the time the sheriff of the place and came with all the posse, the understanding is seized and taken with the object it introduces, as if it had a legal right to be alone considered there."[33]

Almost as strong as the link between deliberation and governance is the link between habit and governance. The two are yoked together both by those who denigrate habit and by those who celebrate it, the first seeing habit as resulting in tyrannical governance, the second seeing habit as responsible for governance in its benignly effective workings. The opening sentence of Montaigne's essay on custom tells the story—one that will later reappear in Locke[34]—about the village woman who lifted a calf each day from its infancy onward and found that eventually she could still lift the animal even after it had grown to be an ox. On the face of it, this seems to be a story about the extraordinary enabling power of daily habit. Surprisingly, in a not uncharacteristic nonsequitur, Montaigne writes in the very next sentence: "For in truth habit is a violent and treacherous schoolmistress . . . furious and tyrannical."[35] Later in the same essay he writes, "But the principal effect of the power of custom is to seize and ensnare us in such a way that it is hardly within our power . . . to reflect and reason about its ordinances."[36]

It is because habit exerts such "force" that it is credited as governing, whether by celebrators or detractors: "The nature of habit," writes John Dewey, "is to be assertive, insistent, self-perpetuating."[37] Habits are "demands for certain kinds of activities . . . they will . . . they form . . . they furnish . . . they rule."[38] Montaigne himself in the course of his essay shifts from perceiving custom as tyrannizing to custom as governing: "Pindar calls her, so I have been told, the queen and empress of the world."[39] He continues a short time later, "Let us return to the sovereignty of custom." Montaigne's essay ends with his famous warning not against disobeying the law (that would be unthinkable) but even against merely making a suggestion that the law be amended![40] Montaigne throughout this essay is using the word "custom" both for everyday behaviors and for law. While law is a form of habit (regularizing and making customary certain procedures and rules), laws also act to inscribe habits in us, as has been recognized from Aristotle forward: "Legislators make the citizens good by forming habits in them, and this is the wish of every legislator; and those who do not effect it miss their mark, and it is in this that a good constitution differs from a bad one."[41]

Deliberation, like Habit, Entails Material Impediments

Habit is closely associated with materialization. Among the thinkers cited earlier, it was perhaps in the work of William James that the materiality of habit was most strikingly in evidence, since he pictures a mental habit as it takes shape in the material of the brain and likens the event to the process a physical object under-goes, when a dress folds more easily the second time, a violin acquires attributes of the musician who plays it, or a key used nightly turns smoothly in its lock. The emergency procedures looked at throughout this book often take an externalized or materialized form: a written and memorized rule about count-ing, an emergency kit, a fallout shelter with thick walls and a ventilation system, a written contract with the specification of a twenty-foot ladder to be brought to the disaster site and the name of the person who will carry it there. Quite apart from the presence of any literal form of materialization, the sheer "force" of habit, described by Montaigne and Dewey, gives it its quality of "substantiveness" as though it were a *physical* presence. That substantiveness certainly constrains our freedom; if a friend's heart stops, the person who has learned CPR does not do any one of the hundred inventive things he might otherwise have done (flail his arms about, run for help, cry, shake the afflicted person, cover him with kisses) but begins to move through a very confined set of actions. The same is true in every other case; even the dress could be said to have lost its freedom to fall into the hundred configurations open to it before it acquired the habit of folding. Having internalized the habit, as Montaigne complains, we lose our freedom and "no longer have the liberty of even raising our eyes."

Deliberation, too, entails just such a loss of liberty, as the word itself—de-liberation—announces. Thomas Hobbes makes the point unmistakable: "And it is called Deliberation, because it is a putting an end to the Liberty we had of doing, or omitting, according to our Appetite, or Aversion."[42] Brilliant and deeply crediting accounts of the material encumbrance of deliberation are provided by John Locke, on the one hand, and by John Dewey and Charles Peirce on the other.

Throughout *Conduct of the Understanding*, Locke criticizes rapid and unrestrained thinking, complaining that speech usually outpaces thinking, and thinking outpaces evidence.[43] The mind has a fast forward momentum that makes it skip from one part of knowledge to another without "due examination of particulars."[44] This forward momentum is a species of "laziness" which allows the mind to take the first object that comes along. Locke calls this rapidity a state of "prostituting the mind" because the mind gives itself to the first comer.[45] It then wanders off to another subject, then another, then another.[46]

When Locke speaks of "well-grounded arguments" he has physical ground in mind. In his argument against haste he speaks of one who rides through a country, acquiring a

> loose description of here a mountain and there a plain, here a morass and there a river . . . Such superficial ideas and observations as these he may collect in galloping over it. But the more useful observations of the soil, plants, animals and inhabitants, with their several sorts and properties, must necessarily escape him; and it is seldom men ever discover the rich mines without some digging. Nature commonly lodges her treasure and jewels in rocky ground. If the matter be knotty and the sense lies deep, *the mind must stop and buckle to it, and stick upon it* with labour, and thought, and close contemplation.[47]

Objects of thought have weight, and are elsewhere, as here, described in terms of physical ground. Locke even develops a term for thinking that arrives at evidentiary and weighted objects; he calls it "bottoming." In a section devoted to reading,

Locke says one must go through the encumbering process of locating where the argument "bottoms," a process that is so thick that it will at first be experienced as a "clog" in one's studies, a word he repeats admiringly several times.[48] The instruction to see where "the argument bottoms" may seem offhand in the section on reading, but late in the book "bottoming" becomes a formal term to which a special section is devoted: "Section 44: Bottoming." He illustrates the aspiration to find where any issue or question "bottoms" with the idea of the equality of all men, a certainty which can be carried reliably through all debates and questions.[49]

This same vision of material encumbrance is central to the accounts of deliberation given by Dewey and, earlier, by Peirce. In *How We Think*, Dewey outlines the sequence of steps entailed in deliberation. It begins with the "felt-experience" of a difficulty, a state of "undefined uneasiness" or "perplexity." This perception of unease leads to an interruption in one's normal action, whether physical of mental. Deliberation is an interruption and a search for an object to restore the forward momentum.[50] This state of suspended motion is uncomfortable, even painful, and is therefore one which must be "endured"; one must resist easy or arbitrary suggestions that would let one return prematurely to the "inertia" of forward "gliding" motion.[51] One mentally tries out various possibilities, conducting a series of mental experiments; because the solutions are carried out in the imagination only, the consequences are "not final or fatal" as they would be if actually enacted.[52] Eventually this mental testing enables one to find an object which releases one from the uncomfortable state of deliberation.

Charles Peirce provides a strikingly similar account of deliberation, describing the act of thinking as motivated "by the irritation of doubt," an uncomfortable state which is only "appeased" once the act of thinking finds an appropriate object of belief, which in turn leads to "the establishment in our nature of a rule of action, or, say for short, a *habit*."[53] Both Peirce and Dewey mean their accounts to apply across a wide range of instances that includes everyday acts such as deciding which path to take when the road forks or whether to pay one's transportation fare with the five coppers or the nickel one has just pulled from one's pocket.[54]

But the opposite end of the spectrum, where emergency and survival are at stake, is clearly crucial. "Now, the identity of a habit," Peirce writes, "depends on how it might lead us to act, not merely under such circumstances as are likely to arise, but under such as might possibly occur, no matter how improbable they may be."[55] For improbable events where deliberation is especially crucial, we develop forms of what Peirce calls "self-notification"[56] and what the later theorist Jon Elster calls "self-binding."[57] Dewey writes:

> By thought man also develops and arranges artificial signs to remind him in advance of consequences, and of ways of securing and avoiding them. . . . [C]ivilized man deliberately *makes* such signs; he sets up in advance of wreckage warning buoys, and builds lighthouses where he sees signs that such events may occur. . . . The very essence of civilized culture is that we deliberately erect monuments and memorials, lest we forget; and deliberately institute, in advance of the happening of various contingencies and emergencies of life, devices for detecting their approach and registering their nature, for warding off what is unfavorable, or at least for protecting ourselves from its full impact . . .[58]

Dewey's buoys, lighthouses, monuments, and memorials of deliberation are what Elster means by forms of self-binding or pre-commitment in which "we temporarily deposit our will in some external structure" until "after some time [it] returns to its source and modifies our behavior"; capable of both rationality and irrationality, we invent forms of self-binding to "protect [ourselves] against the irrationality."[59] Dewey's general account of deliberation serves well as an account of the Swiss shelter system, the Saskatchewan social contracts, the transnational rules for CPR, and—of greatest importance here—the constitutional requirements overseeing the United States's entry into war, the channel markers and lighthouses that mark out a highly specific and constrained path into war. To sail outside those channel markers may feel like freedom, but we are careening into an abyss that places the entire earth in peril.

CONCLUSION

Emergency procedures are laden with deliberation. There may well, as we have seen, be a long temporal hiatus between the deliberation and the actual enactment of the procedure: the Swiss debate about whether to have a shelter system and the population's actual act of inhabiting the shelters when a nuclear weapon is fired. The fact that there is a temporal interruption between the deliberation and the performance of the action does not mean that the final action—the inhabiting of the shelters—was nondeliberative, nonvolitional, outside the population's will or choice. Aristotle says choice is "what has been decided [by] previous deliberation"; a choice is "that which is chosen before other things."[60] Of course, deliberation may be strikingly visible both in the creation and in the enactment stages; deliberation may be not only the path by which the emergency procedure was arrived at but also the specified content of that procedure. That is precisely the case in the United States's requirement for a congressional declaration of war, a provision debated and determined at the country's constitutional convention and one whose very content stipulates the action of debate and voting by a large assembly of people. Of the four models of emergency procedure, the deliberative act remains most visible in the provision for a declaration of war; but the capacity for ongoing deliberation is part of what is being protected in all four. The key point here, however, is that each of the four—CPR, the Swiss shelter system, the constitutional provision for a congressional declaration, and the Canadian or Ethiopian or Japanese social contracts for shared rescue—is the outcome of a deliberative process, and all are objects of choice.

Aristotle lists the things that *cannot* be objects of deliberation: 1) the elementary, 2) heavenly movements such as the solstice, 3) arbitrary things that could just as easily be something else, 4) objects of deliberation for other populations—that is, things indeed arrived at by deliberation but not by one's own deliberation, and 5) impossibilities. What makes the Swiss shelter system an instance of Venturi-esque throbbing Technicolor ingenuity is that, though Switzerland conceives of itself as having almost no influence on the superpowers, and though it acknowledges that geographically speaking it could well be in the direct or indirect line of fire, it conceives of the survival of its population as an object of deliberation, not as an impossibility. And what is disheartening about the disavowal of our own emergency preparation in the Constitution is that it takes our fate out of the sphere of deliberation and designates it either an impossibility, a phenomenon akin to the solstice, an arbitrary thing, or an outcome to be determined by another population.

It is the argument of this book that the two constitutional provisions overseeing our entry into war provide the best possible protection for our democracy, protection against—among many other things—monarchic weapons, whether the nuclear form of monarchic weaponry invented in the 1940s or some future form of monarchic weaponry invented in the 2040s. Some people may wish to argue that these two constitutional provisions (and their equivalents in other countries) have flaws and that we need to amend the Constitution to provide some other, better form of protection. If so, the conclusions we can reach about thinking in an emergency need to be kept in mind. First, because technology makes what was once the mere ritual ceremony of monarchy a concrete reality backed by genocidal killing power (the capacity to annihilate vast populations at will), civil society is in a new situation and has to secure appropriate laws and procedures that make the return of monarchy impossible. Second, these procedures must be as explicit as the CPR protocol or the Swiss shelter system with its extraordinary specification for Saint Roch, his dog, and the heart-shaped ceramic Eucharist wafer the dog holds in its mouth. Third, this kind of specificity is the only resource that has been shown to work in medicine, in floods, in search and rescue missions, or in any context of injury from the present back through history to the tales of Thucydides and Aesop and Aristotle. Inventing these and making sure they are widely understood—understood by the entire population—is one of the philosophic and civic responsibilities of our age.

NOTES

Preface

1 Rae Langton, conversation, May 30, 2010.

2 On the treatment of newspapers, see W. A. Veenhoven, who states that even quotations from speeches in Parliament were prohibited; at first newspapers would leave large white spaces to indicate that material had been censored, but soon white spaces were prohibited (*Case Studies on Human Rights and Fundamental Freedoms: A World Survey*, vol. 5 [The Hague: Nijhoff, 1975–76], 497). On the jailing of the opposition, including "700 national leaders of her political opposition," see Murray J. Leaf, *Pragmatism and Development: The Prospect for Pluralistic Transformation in the Third World* (Westport, CT: Bergin & Garvey, 1998), 31. On "coerced sterilization," see James G. Chadney, "Family Planning: India's Achilles' Heel?" in *India: The Years of Indira Gandhi*, ed. Y. K. Malik and D. K. Vajpeyi (Leiden, Netherlands: E. J. Brill, 1988), 92.

Chapter One: The Seduction to Stop Thinking

1 Clinton L. Rossiter, *Constitutional Dictatorship: Crisis Government in the Modern Democracies* (Princeton: Princeton University Press, 1948).

2 Hans Born, "National Governance of Nuclear Weapons: Opportunities and Constraints," Geneva Center for the Democratic

Control of Armed Forces (DCAF), Policy Paper No. 15, 2007. North Korea conducted its first nuclear test in 2006, but according to the Federation of American Scientists, its status as a nuclear state is still unclear in 2010.

3 These 2010 weapons figures, as well as those in the next sentence, are reported by SIPRI Yearbook, Bulletin of Atomic Scientists, and the Federation of American Scientists.

4 Born, "National Governance of Nuclear Weapons," 7, 12.

5 Ibid., 12.

6 The most detailed documentary account of the path along which US presidents assumed formal control of nuclear weapons is Frank G. Klotz's unpublished Oxford D.Phil dissertation, "The US President and the Control of Strategic Nuclear Weapons" (1980). Lt. Gen. Klotz is currently the commander of Air Force Global Strike Command and hence oversees all the country's intercontinental ballistic missiles and nuclear-capable B-2 and B-52 bombers. For the case at the International Court of Justice, see "Legality of the Threat or Use of Nuclear Weapons," Advisory Opinion, 1996, ICJ, 226 (July 8).

7 Born, "National Governance of Nuclear Weapons," 5, 13.

8 Jules Lobel, "Emergency Power and the Decline of Liberalism," *Yale Law Journal* 98 (May 1980), 1401, 1404, 1408, 1418, 1420, 1416.

9 Following the shooting of President Reagan, Secretary of State Alexander Haig's public announcement, "I am in control here," was treated as a spectacular personal blunder. In fact, it exposed before the eyes of the nation—had we only understood what we were seeing—the extraordinary shift in the line of presidential succession that has come about through nonconstitutional means. The Twenty-Fifth Amendment to the Constitution requires that presidential authority move from the president, to the vice president, to the speaker of the House, to the president pro tem of the Senate, and then to the secretary of state. But the Reagan administration had also arranged for a military line of succession—or what Haig and others repeatedly referred to on the day of the shooting as

a "crisis management" line of succession, renamed the "national command authority" a day later—that went from the president to the vice president to (skipping the House and Senate, and even the civil Cabinet member, the secretary of state) the secretary of defense. In fact, some accounts of this new line of national command succession indicate that the line goes directly from the president to the secretary of defense. Hence, there was a consciously designed split between constitutional or civilian lines of authority and military lines of authority. Evidence suggests a third line of succession for controlling the nuclear codes and, therefore, firing atomic weapons. As secretary of state, Alexander Haig was not "in control here" according to *any* of the three lines of succession, but the existence of three contradictory lines makes explicable Haig's own confusion about the matter. Press attention to Haig's "blunder" (and to his personal conflict with Secretary of Defense Caspar Weinberger) deflected attention from the far more astonishing and damaging revelation that secret, nonconstitutional lines of succession had been created that preempted the constitutional, popularly endorsed, and publicly recognized sequence.

For accounts of the shooting, Haig's announcement, and the constitutional and "crisis management" lines of succession, see the *New York Times*, March 31, 1981, and April 1, 1981. For nonconstitutional lines of succession authorizing the firing of nuclear weapons, see House of Representatives, Subcommittee on International Security and Scientific Affairs of the Committee on International Relations, *First Use of Nuclear Weapons: Preserving Responsible Control*, 94th Cong., 2d sess., March 1976, 39, 42, 76, 79, 128, 213, 215.

10 Born, "National Governance of Nuclear Weapons," 15.

11 Peter Hennessy, *The Secret State: Whitehall and the Cold War* (London: Allen Lane, 2002), 105, quoting Public Records Office, DEFE 25/49, "Nuclear Retaliation Procedures," Report from GEN 743/10 (Revise), 23 January 1962. The record does not indicate who appoints the deputies. The use of the word "retaliation"

here and elsewhere in Hennessy's book should not mislead one into thinking that Britain has a second-use policy; what is being "retaliated" against in some of these papers is not an incoming nuclear weapon but a land army marching across Europe. (See the description of Operation VISITATION, 186.)

12 On the breaking of national and international law during the administration of George W. Bush, see Elaine Scarry, *Rule of Law, Misrule of Men* (Cambridge, MA: MIT Press, 2010). On the extensive use of a private presidential army during the Bush administration, see Jeremy Scahill's analysis of private contractors in the US wars in Iraq and Afghanistan, as well as in New Orleans following Hurricane Katrina in *Blackwater: The Rise of the World's Most Powerful Mercenary Army* (New York: Nation Books, 2007).

13 As I show in *The Body in Pain* (New York: Oxford University Press, 1985, 139–57), nuclear war conforms to the model of torture, not the model of war.

14 Aristotle, *De Anima (On the Soul)*, trans. and introd. Hugh Lawson-Tancred (New York: Penguin, 1986), section 434a, 216. Tancred sees the distinction between perception and deliberation as the central contribution of Chapter 11 to the doctrines presented earlier in *De Anima*. Bruce Aune states the Aristotelian opposition clearly in "Thinking," *Encyclopedia of Philosophy*, vol. 7, ed. Paul Edwards (New York: Macmillan Publishing, 1967), 100.

15 Aesop, "An Unseasonable Reproof," in *Fables of Aesop*, trans. S. A. Handford (New York: Penguin, 1954), 197.

16 Charles Baudelaire, "Le Cygne," in Baudelaire, *Selected Verse with an Introduction and Prose Translations by Francis Scarfe* (New York: Penguin, 1961), 210.

17 Thucydides, *History of the Peloponnesian War*, trans. Rex Warner (New York: Penguin, 1954), 152.

18 Ibid., 154.

19 Ibid., 155.

20 The laws of most countries accord a special status to dying words. In Anglo-American law, for example, hearsay is ordinar-

ily inadmissible in court, but it becomes admissible if the hearsay is spoken by someone murdered who, before dying, names the murderer; see Karl S. Guthke, *Last Words: Variations on a Theme in Cultural History* (Princeton: Princeton University Press, 1992), 28. While dying words permit a loosening of legal constraints, a tightening of constraints may instead arise as illustrated in two other genres of language—whistleblowing (laws protecting whistle-blowers suffered a setback in the 2006 Supreme Court decision in *Garcetti v. Ceballos*) and political dissent in wartime (the 1919 case *Schenck v. United States* was the first to address, and then deny, the applicability of First Amendment speech to wartime dissent; writing for a unanimous court, Oliver Wendell Holmes argued that obstructing war conscription, as Schenck had done in a pamphlet urging that "A conscript is little better than a convict," presented a clear danger analogous to "crying fire in a theatre").

21 Sylvain Ayotte, "Emergency Preparedness in Quebec: Co-ordinated Response among Partners," *Emergency Preparedness Digest*, October–December 1991, 2.

22 Artaud does not, however, explicitly name Thucydides. Marseilles, the region of France from which Artaud comes, itself has a tradition of plague writing dating back to the 1720 plague in Provence, a set of writings investigated by historian Daniel Gordon in "The City and the Plague in the Age of Enlightenment," *Yale French Studies* 92 (1997), 77–78.

23 Antonin Artaud, *Theatre and its Double*, trans. Mary Caroline Richards (New York: Grove, 1958), 92.

24 Ibid., 82.

25 An everyday habit may in some cases even accelerate an emergency. A study in the 1970s attempted to explain why so many of those raped or robbed were teachers or nurses. The study concluded that the victims were disproportionately people who had habits of serving or helping others. The criminal attack often began with a request for help: the attacker would ask for the time, for a street direction, for a match, or some other form of assis-

tance. People in the habit of helping strangers were therefore at risk. Such a revelation does not mean a librarian should stop helping strangers, but that she should abstain from helping strangers if she is walking alone on a street that is otherwise unpopulated.

26 Donald L. Metz, *Running Hot: Structure and Stress in Ambulance Work* (Cambridge, MA: Abt Books, 1981), 145.

Chapter Two: Four Models of Emergency Thinking

1 A. Ocklitz, "Cardiopulmonary resuscitation already in Egypt 5,000 years ago?" *Wiener Klinische Wochenschrift* 109, no. 11 (June 1997), 406–12.

2 2 Kings 4: 34–35, cited in Mickey S. Eisenberg, *Life in the Balance: Emergency Medicine and the Quest to Reverse Sudden Death* (New York: Oxford University Press, 1977), 35.

3 Eisenberg, *Life in the Balance*, 55–136.

4 A. Olotu et al., "Characteristics and outcome of cardiopulmonary resuscitation in hospitalized African children," *Resuscitation* 80, no. 1 (2009), 69–72.

5 52% of the children were younger than one year; 44% were between one and five years old; 18% were six to fourteen years old. (Ibid., 70.)

6 A 22% survival rate (eighteen of eighty-two children) rather than the earlier 15% figure. (Ibid., 71.)

7 The age would be younger if all patients had been included. Cardiac arrest patients younger than fifteen were eliminated from the study at the outset.

8 I. Desalu and O. T. Kushimo, "An audit of perioperative cardiac arrest at Lagos University Teaching Hospital," *Nigerian Journal of Clinical Practice* 10, no. 3 (September 2007), 188–93; and I. Desalu, O. T. Kushimo, and O. Akinlaja, "Adherence to CPR guidelines during perioperative cardiac arrest in a developing country," *Resuscitation* 69, no. 3 (2006), 517–20. The second of

these two articles focuses exclusively on the need for conformity to guidelines, not introducing the problem of blood loss.

9 Kilifi District Hospital has no equipment for ventilation or defibrillation, so both breathing and compression were done by the physicians and nurses directly. In Lagos Hospital, the breathing part of CPR was given by manual ventilation.

10 Peter Safar and Martin McMahon, *Resuscitation of the Unconscious Victim: A Manual for Rescue Breathing*, 18, 19.

11 A test in which viewers were asked to reproduce the curl of a hand depicted in a photograph, a tracing of a photograph, and a cartoon sketch is described in E. H. Gombrich, Julian Hochberg, and Max Black, *Art, Perception, and Reality* (Baltimore: Johns Hopkins University Press, 1972), 35, 74, 78. Gombrich, Hochberg, and Black argue that cartoon is the opposite of camouflage because it provides an exaggeration of the body that matches the way the body exaggerates inner states, magnifying a small bump into the felt experience of a large one.

12 Safar and McMahon, *Resuscitation*, 71. The instruction to "watch the chest" is at least as crucial in giving chest compressions as in assisting the victim's breathing. In its 2010 guidelines, the American Heart Association stresses the importance of compressing the chest of an adult 100 times per minute to a depth of two inches and watching to make sure the chest fully recoils between each compression (co-chairs John M. Field, Mary Fran Hazinski, et al., "2010 American Heart Association Guidelines for Cardiopulmonary Resuscitation and Emergency Cardiovascular Care Science," *Circulation* 122 [November 18, 2010], 640–56).

13 W. A. Carlo et al., "Educational impact of the neonatal resuscitation program in low-risk delivery centers in a developing country," *Journal of Pediatrics* 154, no. 4 (April 2009), 504–8.

14 Olotu et al., "Characteristics . . . in hospitalized African children," 72, italics added. The protocol followed in Kilifi is the Pediatric Advanced Life Support of the Resuscitation Council, UK. The American Heart Association's November 2010 guidelines acknowl-

edge that the interval for retraining it had earlier recommended—twelve to twenty-four months—is too long, given that "knowledge and skills . . . decline within weeks after initial . . . training." It has not yet arrived at a new recommendation, but it may well approximate the three-to-six-month interval urged by the Zambia study described above (co-chairs Mary Fran Hazinski, Jerry P. Nolan, et al., "2010 International Cardiopulmonary Resuscitation and Emergency Cardiovascular Care Science with Treatment Recommendations," *Circulation* 122 [October 2010], 250–75).

15 Stephanie Rosborough, MD, conversation, March 11, 2010.

16 American Heart Association, "2002 Heart and Stroke Statistical Update," Dallas, 2002.

17 Safar and McMahon, *Resuscitation*, 5. The figures on oxygen loss given here were based on the extensive experiments Safar had conducted. Eisenberg's 1997 book specifies that permanent brain dramage begins four minutes after oxygen is cut off (*Life in the Balance*, 14).

18 R. Vukmir, "Witnessed arrest, but not delayed bystander cardiopulmonary resuscitation improves prehospital cardiac survival," *Emergency Medicine Journal* 21, no. 3 (May 2004), 370–73.

19 Safar and McMahon, *Resuscitation*, 12. Safar notes that expired breath actually contains 18% oxygen if the rescuer is taking deep breaths, as is urged in the protocol.

20 Eisenberg, *Life in the Balance*, 92, 93, 101.

21 See the copyright page of the handbook.

22 When Safar moved to the University of Pittsburgh Hospital in 1968 to establish a Department of Anesthesiology, he set up a paramedic service (called Freedom House) in the city's Hill district, where the greatest number of the city's African-American population lived (Eisenberg, *Life in the Balance*, 103). It is widely credited as the first advanced medical emergency program in the country, and spread to many other cities.

23 Eisenberg, *Life in the Balance*, 127. In fact, there are other points in the story when distribution precedes and assists medical discov-

ery. For example, Elam's initial work on artificial respiration began when he was walking through the polio ward of the University of Minnesota Hospital in 1946, saw a young girl who had turned blue being rushed through the corridor, and interrupted their rush to deliver mouth-to-nose resuscitation which immediately transformed her from blue to pink. He knew how to do this because he had the night before read a book cataloguing eighty-four historical techniques of resuscitation, and recalled the description of midwives delivering mouth-to-nose breaths to newborns, a procedure scorned as "vulgar" by the medical profession (85–90).

24 Kouwenhoven cited ibid., 126.

25 David Segal, "A Reader's Digest that Grandma Never Dreamed Of," *New York Times*, December 19, 2009.

26 Eisenberg, *Life in the Balance*, 128.

27 Gary Lombardi, E. John Gallagher, and Paul Gennis, "Outcome of Out-of-Hospital Cardiac Arrest in New York City," *JAMA* 271, no. 9 (March 1994), 678–83.

28 Marc Eckstein, Samuel J. Stratton, and Linda S. Chan, "Cardiac Arrest Resuscitation Evaluation in Los Angeles: CARE–LA," *Annals of Emergency Medicine* 45, no. 5 (2005), 504–9.

29 Mikael Holmberg et al., "Survival after cardiac arrest outside hospital in Sweden," *Resuscitation* 36 (1998), 29–36.

30 Lombardi et al., "Outcome . . . in New York City," 679.

31 L. B. Becker, "Outcome of CPR in a large metropolitan area—where are the survivors?" *Annals of Emergency Medicine* 20, no. 4 (1991), 355–61.

32 C. Stein, "Out-of-hospital cardiac arrest cases in Johannesburg, South Africa: a first glimpse of short-term outcomes from a paramedic clinical learning base," *Emergency Medicine Journal* 26 (2009), 670–74, esp. 673 comparing Los Angeles and Johannesburg figures for return of spontaneous circulation (ROSC).

33 Ibid., 673.

34 Bystanders assisted in 28% of the cases in Los Angeles and Sweden, and 32% of the cases in New York City.

35 The study of Sweden, for example, cites studies documenting sur-
    vival rates of between 14% and 18% in Seattle, Washington, and
    King County, Washington, and 17% in Helsinki. The elapsed time
    between cardiac arrest and defibrillation in Seattle was three to four
    minutes. (Holmberg et al., "Survival . . . in Sweden," 33, 34.

36 Taku Iwami et al., "Continuous Improvements in 'Chain of Sur-
    vival' Increased Survival after Out-of-Hospital Cardiac Arrests:
    A Large-Scale Population-Based Study," *Circulation* 119 (2009),
    728–34. Prior to the surge of citizen training, Osaka's survival
    rate had been 5%.

37 Tetsuhisa Kitamura et al., "Conventional and chest-compression-
    only cardiopulmonary resuscitation by bystanders for children
    who have out-of-hospital cardiac arrests: a prospective, nation-
    wide, population-based cohort study," *Lancet*, March 2010, 1–8.

38 Ibid., 2, 4.

39 Ibid., 4.

40 Ibid., 5, 6.

41 Jonathan R. Cole, *The Great American University: Its Rise to Preemi-
    nence; Its Indispensable National Role; Why It Must Be Protected* (New
    York: Public Affairs, 2009), 237.

42 American Heart Association, report of the "2005 International
    Consensus Conference on Cardiopulmonary Resuscitation and
    Emergency Cardiovascular Care Science with Treatment Recom-
    mendations," *Circulation* 112 (2005). The 2010 guidelines make it
    clear why an untrained bystander can use compression-only when
    resuscitating adults but should use classic CPR when resuscitat-
    ing children. While heart attacks in most adults are initiated by
    ventricular fibrillation, "the majority of pediatric cardiac arrests are
    asphyxial, with only 5% to 15% attributable to VF [ventricular
    fibrillation]" (Field, Hazinski, et al., "2010 American Heart Associ-
    ation Guidelines"). Supplying breath is therefore as crucial as com-
    pressing the heart, as is also true in cases where an adult's cardiac
    arrest has been caused by asphyxia (for example, near drowning).

43 M. R. Sayre et al., "Hands-only (compression-only) cardiopul-

monary resuscitation: a call to action for bystander response to adults who experience out-of-hospital sudden cardiac arrest. A science advisory for the public from the American Heart Association Emergency Cardiovascular Care Committee," *Circulation* 117 (2008), 2162–67.

44 Amsterdam reported 150 resuscitations in four years (Eisenberg, *Life in the Balance*, 14, 59, 61). Eisenberg is himself a physician and medical researcher. His articles on bystander CPR are cited in the bibliographies of many of the journal articles on bystanders cited above.

45 Eisenberg (ibid., 3) provides this number, based on sixty beats per minute.

46 Article 2, "Quill Plains (Naicam) Mutual Aid Area" (signed December 1, 1986); and Article 9a, "Battlefords Mutual Aid Area" (Signed August 29, 1988).

47 Each contract lists the population size of the participating regions.

48 Bill 54, "An Act Respecting Emergency" (*Statutes of Saskatchewan, 1989–90*, ch. E–8.1, also called the Emergency Planning Act).

49 Former mayor Dorothy Saunderson, conversation, April 24, 2010. The mayor, who served in that office for twenty-five years, was eighty-five years old at the time of the flood. Some reports place the total rainfall in the area closer to fifteen than to thirteen inches.

50 Fraser Hunter et al., "Interagency Report on the Torrential Rainstorm of July 3, 2000 at Vanguard, Saskatchewan," Canada–Saskatchewan Memorandum of Understanding on Water Committee (July 2003), 3, 11.

51 Saunderson, conversation. As Mayor Saunderson's husband was gravely ill, the declaratory act was carried out by the deputy mayor.

52 Fraser G. Hunter, et al., "The Vanguard Torrential Storm (Meteorology and Hydrology)," *Canadian Water Resources Journal* 27, no. 2 (Summer 2002), 213, 223.

53 Ibid., 222–23, 219–20.

54 Carl Friske, emergency management advisor, Saskatchewan Emergency Planning Office, conversations, May 10, 11, 2010. Carl Friske, who arrived by boat on the first day and coordinated public works, social services, and public information for the first twelve days, was the only official present from the Emergency Planning Office. All other labor was carried out by residents and volunteers whose work he describes with quiet amazement.

55 Ibid.

56 D. B. Donald et al., "Mobilization of Pesticides on an Agricultural Landscape Flooded by a Torrential Storm," *Environmental Toxicology & Chemistry* 24, no. 1 (January, 2005), 10.

57 Friske, conversations, May 2010.

58 Saunderson, conversation.

59 Ibid.

60 The "Interagency Report on the Torrential Rainstorm" stresses the importance of this form of distributing information on 11, 16, and 18 (recommendations 3, quoted above, and 5 on the use of, but non-reliance on, ordinary forms of media).

61 I am grateful to John A. Woltman and Carl Friske of Saskatchewan Community Services for sending me copies of the Battlefords and Quill Plains social contracts and regional maps of "Municipal Mutual Aid Areas" and "Provincial Emergency Planning Districts," as well as for their verbal descriptions by telephone in February 1993 and September 1995.

62 Gary Storey, "Grain Elevators," *The Encyclopedia of Saskatchewan*, www.esask.uregina.ca/.

63 Michael Cottrell, "History of Saskatchewan," *The Encyclopedia of Saskatchewan.*

64 Gary Storey, "Grain Elevators." See also Nora Russell's article on "Co-operatives" in this same online volume.

65 "Naicam EMO [Emergency Measures Organization] Co-ordinator Report on Sask Wheat Pool Elevator Fire in Naicam on April 18/19." My thanks to John A. Woltman for sending me the formal report on the 1990 Naicam fire and for speaking with me by phone.

66 Mike Steers, "The Elevator's on Fire," *Emergency Preparedness Digest*, July–September 1990, 10, 11.

67 Ibid., 11. The name of the lake and the number of trucks is given in the "Naicam EMO Co-ordinator Report," 1.

68 "Naicam EMO Co-ordinator Report," 1.

69 Steers, "The Elevator's on Fire," 11. The after-action report says "the town crew" reported 87,000 gallons (395,500 liters)available at 11:20, 91,000 at 12:10, and 63,000 "on hand" at 3 p.m.

70 John Woltman, conversation, September 25, 1995.

71 Friske, conversations, May 2010.

72 Though the test was three years in the making, it cost the province only $8,000 (Canadian), in part because so much of the labor was volunteer. Mike Theilmann, "The Little Exercise that Grew," *Emergency Preparedness Digest*, July–September 1990, 16–19.

73 1989 Saskatchewan Emergency Planning Act (amended and updated 1992, 1993, 1998, 2002, and 2003). See Sections 15.1.a,b, and c; 18.1.f, j, k; 21.1.a.iv, vii, viii, and x, for the potentially problematic provisions, as well as the accompanying provisions that place restrictions on these emergency powers.

74 Following Hurricane Andrew in 1992, the governors of southern states formed a mutual aid plan called EMAC, the Emergency Management Assistance Compact, which the US Congress made a public law in 1996. As EMAC's website notes, it is "the first national disaster compact since the Civil Defense Compact of 1950 to be ratified by Congress." While this is surely an important step, the number of citizens who have heard of EMAC appears to be small. Further, even those who know the term will find a website most of whose categories are unenterable because they are password-protected: "EMAC Operation Manual," "Forms and Checklists," "Notice and Reporting Systems," and many others are off-limits to the public. Some helpful-sounding categories such as "EMAC Mission Ready Package for up to 25 Personnel," "EMAC Mission Ready Package for 50 Personnel" and other mission ready packages for up to 1,500 personnel can be opened by anyone, but

the mission ready package is only a five-page form with fill-in-the-blanks for items such as "Resource Provider/Agency" and space for projected costs of items such as air travel, per diem food costs, and vehicle costs for state officials traveling to another state. Approximately three-quarters of an inch of space is provided in which to describe the mission purpose and constraints.

75 Robert Pekkanen, *Japan's Dual Civil Society: Member without Advocates* (Stanford: Stanford University Press, 2006), 133, 135.

76 Ibid., 88.

77 Ibid., 94.

78 Alexis de Tocqueville, *Democracy in America*, trans. Henry Reeve, Francis Bowen, Phillips Bradley (New York: Vintage, 1960), vol. 1, 310.

79 Tocqueville, *Democracy in America*, vol. 2, 114, 115.

80 Pekkanen, *Japan's Dual Civil Society*, 96, 102.

81 Tocqueville, *Democracy in America*, vol. 2, 117.

82 Pekkanen, *Japan's Dual Civil Society*, 133–36.

83 Goran Hyden, *No Shortcuts to Progress: African Development Management in Perspective* (Berkeley, CA: University of California Press, 1983), 6–32.

84 Michael Bratton, "Beyond the State: Civil Society and Associational Life in Africa," *World Politics* 41, no. 3 (1989), 411.

85 Kenneth Little, *West African Urbanization: A Study of Voluntary Associations in Social Change* (Cambridge: Cambridge University Press, 1965), 26, 27, 34, 48.

86 Ibid., 26, 27. Those associations that appeared to be based on the former village were often so open to people from other places that Little judges the place name to be quasi-fictional; on the other hand, he shows that migrants often sent money back to the home village.

87 Ibid., 48.

88 Clifford Geertz, "The Rotating Credit Association: A 'Middle Ring' in Development," *Economic Development and Cultural Change* 10, no. 3, cited in Little, *West African Urbanization*, 51.

89 Shirley Ardener, *The Comparative Study of Rotating Credit Associations*, unpublished ms., cited in Little, *West African Urbanization*, 51, n. 1. After the publication of Little's book, Ardener's study was published (and is therefore available) in *Journal of the Royal Anthropological Institute of Great Britain and Ireland* 94, no. 2 (July–December 1964), 201–29.

90 Shawn J. McGuire, "Vulnerability in Farmer Seed Systems: Farmer Practices for coping with Seed Insecurity for Sorghum in Eastern Ethiopia," *Economic Botany* 61, no. 3 (Autumn 2007), 21, 215–16, 219. McGuire explains that the NGOs themselves have limited seed and have to give it to those who have enough wealth to promise that the sowing will be done by a specific date, a promise a farmer who has no oxen cannot make since he must wait to sow until the unscheduled day when a neighboring farmer can provide him with oxen.

91 Michael Bratton, "Drought, Food and the Social Organization of Small Farmers in Zimbabwe," in *Drought and Hunger in Africa: Denying Famine a Future,* ed. Michael H. Glantz (Cambridge: Cambridge University Press, 1987), 224, 225, 239.

92 Ibid., 231, 232. One year into the drought, 82% of the farmers reported their belief that the associations had grown stronger; even three years into the drought, 63% still felt they were continuing to strengthen.

93 Ibid., 224.

94 McGuire, "Vulnerability," 218.

95 Here I am speaking about the way voluntary associations address the nation-state (and through the nation-state, the large population), rather than about reverse: the way the nation-state may choose to address the voluntary associations. As became apparent in the description of the Kobai earthquake, a state can encourage or instead discourage civil society by granting or denying legal recognition, tax-exempt status, and low postage rates. More drastically, the state can actively work to suppress civil society, as it did in Ethiopia during the 1974–87 Mengistu regime.

96 Tocqueville, *Democracy in America*, vol. 1, 202.

97 Bratton, "Beyond the State," 417.

98 Robert D. Putnam with Robert Leonardi and Raffaella Y. Nanetti, *Making Democracy Work: Civic Traditions in Modern Italy* (Princeton: Princeton University Press, 1993), 101.

99 Harold Berman, *Law and Revolution: The Formation of the Western Legal Tradition* (Cambridge, MA: Harvard University Press, 1983), 393. Peter Kropotkin describes how in Iceland and Scandinavian lands the entire body of law would be recited aloud before an assembly, in *Mutual Aid: A Factor of Evolution* (New York: McClure Phillips, 1903), 158.

100 Berman, *Law and Revolution*, 375.

101 Henri Pirenne, *Medieval Cities: Their Origins and the Revival of Trade*, trans. Frank D. Halsey (Princeton: Princeton University Press, 1925), 218. For the full contract, see Kropotkin, *Mutual Aid*, 177. Despite their aura of revolution and volatility, the first French communes were brought into being by the desire for self-help: "to protect the town and keep the peace in circumstances where self-help seemed the only hope" (Susan Reynolds, *An Introduction to the History of English Medieval Towns* [Oxford: Clarendon Press, 1977], 104). Reynolds's French sources are A. Vermeesch, "Essai sur les origins et la signification de la commune dans le nord de la France" (Heule, 1966); Petit-Dutaillis, *Les Communes françaises* (Paris, 1947); and P. Michaud-Quantin, *Universitas: Expressions du mouvement communautaire dans le moyen age latin* (Paris, 1970).

102 Berman, *Law and Revolution*, 366.

103 Statute of the *Spade Compagnia*, cited in Putnam, *Making Democracy Work*, 126. Putnam's book shows the startling contemporary relevance of the medieval contracts. Judging the "widening gulf between North and South [to be] the central issue of modern Italian history" (158), he argues that the differences in civic virtue in the two areas correspond precisely with the differences in city contracts in 1300 (Chapter 5) and with mutual aid societies in the 1800s. Not only, then, do mutual aid societies instill habits

to address emergencies, but the very predisposition to form associational groups appears itself to be "a habit" that a given region
practices across many centuries. In his study of civil society in
Japan, Pekkanen cites scholarship showing medieval precedents
for the neighborhood associations, though Pekkanen himself
rejects these precedents (*Japan's Dual Civil Society*, 102–4).

104 According to Pirenne, the word "peace" referred both to freedom
from war and to freedom from crime: "The peace of the city (*pax
villae*) was at the same time the law of the city (*lex villae*)"; "peace"
in the twelfth century "designate[d] the criminal law of the city"
(*Medieval Cities*, 207, 208).

105 Berman, *Law and Revolution*, 396.

106 Putnam, *Making Democracy Work*, 125 (citing Kropotkin, *Mutual
Aid*, 174). Though themselves in need of help, strangers are also
helpful: "information may be obtained [from them] about matters
which one may like to learn."

107 The link between social contract and the wish to eliminate war is
visible in the fact that the social contracts of many different nations
explicitly designate *international* peace a central aspiration, either
in the preamble (e.g., the constitutions of Andorra, Azerbaijan,
Bahrain, Benin, Brazil, Bulgaria, Burkina Faso, Cameroon, Central African Republic, Chad, China, Croatia, Egypt, Germany,
Indonesia, Japan, Oman, Pakistan, Senegal, and Turkey) or in
an early article (e.g., the constitutions of Albania, Angola, Cape
Verde, Ecuador, Finland, Italy, and Laos). It is also the case that
many countries identify *domestic* peace as a central aspiration
in either their preamble (e.g., the constitutions of Cambodia,
Ecuador, Guatemala, Honduras, Laos, Macedonia, Turkey, and
Uganda) or an early article (e.g., the constitutions of Cambodia,
Cameroon, Croatia, Djibouti, Equatorial Guinea, and Ireland).
My thanks to research assistant Matthew Spellberg for patiently
compiling these lists.

108 Federal Office of Civil Defence, *Civil Defence Medical Service*,
Bern, n.d., 4.

109 Federal Office of Civil Defence, *Civil Defence: Figures, Facts, Data, 1989*, Bern, Spring 1989, 505.1. For the repeated assertion that a fallout shelter makes survivability possible even a short distance from the impact, see additional pamphlets published by the Bern office such as *The 1971 Conception of Swiss Civil Defence*, 26.

110 Lecture by David Giri, International Conference on Advanced Electromagnetics, Torino, Italy, September 11, 2001.

111 *Civil Protection Concept: Report of the Federal Council to the Federal Assembly Concerning the New Civil Protection Concept*, Bern, 17 October 2001, v, 23, 24.

112 Ibid., 5, 28.

113 *The 1971 Conception of Swiss Civil Defence*, Bern, 24, 29, italics added.

114 Federal Law on Civil Protection System and Protection & Support Service, 2003, Article 47, 7, 8; and see *Civil Protection Concept*, 24.

115 *Civil Protection Concept*, iii, v, 3, 10, 23.

116 Federal Law on Civil Protection, Articles 11, 13.

117 Federal Law on Civil Protection, Article 15. See also Constitution of Switzerland, Article 61, Clause 3.

118 For the general requirement for "protection of cultural property" (including cultural property that is privately owned) and for "compulsory service," see *Civil Protection Concept*, ii, 10, 13, 17, 24.

119 The 1998 figure is given in *Civil Protection Concept*, 28.

120 See the Federal Office of Civil Protection booklet, *Protection of Cultural Property: A Global Mission*, Bern, 2005, 20.

121 *Protection of Cultural Property*, 5, 13, 14, 18, 21.

122 Iso Camartine, personal conversation at the Institute for Advanced Study in Berlin, April 1990. Iso Camartine is also the friend who described Zürich's Committee on Special Objects.

123 See, for example, *Civil Defence: Figures, Facts, Data, 1989*, 103; *The 1971 Conception of Swiss Civil Defence*, 17; Federal Office of Civil Defence, *Swiss Civil Defence*, Bern, n.d., 3, 6. Article 2 of the Swiss constitution specifies "safeguard[ing] the independence and security of the country" as a main purpose of the constitution.

124 *The 1971 Conception of Swiss Civil Defence*, 47.

125 Paul Hodge, *Washington Post*, January 20, 1977, DC1.

126 "FEMA's Focus Found to be on Armageddon," *St. Petersburg Times*, February 22, 1993, 1A.

127 These narratives all come from the articles of Ted Gup, listed in note 128 below.

128 Gup has almost single-handedly taken on the task of alerting the public to the existence of these shelters. See, for example, Ted Gup, "Doomsday Hideaway," *Time*, December 9, 1991, 26–29; "Underground Government: A Guide to America's Doomsday Bunkers," *Washington Post [Sunday] Magazine*, May 31, 1992, W14; "The Doomsday Blueprints," *Time*, August 10, 1992, 32–39; "How FEMA learned to Stop Worrying about Civilians and Love the Bomb," *Mother Jones*, January–February 1994, 28–31, 74, 76.

129 Ted Gup, "The Ultimate Congressional Hideaway," *Washington Post [Sunday] Magazine*, May 31, 1992, W11. Although Congress was unaware of Greenbrier, it did authorize extravagant funds for the Federal Emergency Management Agency without requiring explanations for how, and on whom, it was being spent.

130 *Civil Defence: Figures, Facts, Data, 1989*, 506, 507.

131 These figures are specified in a July 3, 2009, online report: http://www.swissinfo.ch.

132 *Swiss Civil Defence*, 8, and see notes 111–113 above for both recent and early iterations of the principle.

133 Between 1981 and 1991, when the $2.9 billion mobile presidential shelter was being built, FEMA spent $243 million on preparation "for natural disasters such as hurricanes, earthquakes, and floods" ("FEMA's Focus Found to be on Armageddon"). Ted Gup estimates that each year the government spends less than 50 cents per person on civil defense (*Time*, December 9, 1991). The absence of civil defense preparation during Hurricane Katrina in the fall of 2007 was just one particularly vivid illustration of the ongoing exclusion of the population from the country's conception of "national defense."

Though I have focused here on the extraordinary discrepancy

between executive protection and civilian protection, irrespective of the particular president in office, some presidents have been more concerned about civilian protection than others. For example, Eisenhower used the need to protect the population as a reason for funding a national highway system; Kennedy wanted civilian fallout shelters but Congress refused to fund them ("Civil Defence: Evacuous," *Economist*, November 18, 1978, 20); Carter tried to reactivate civil defense (Richard Burt, "Democrats Back Carter on Nomination Rule," *New York Times*, August 12, 1980, A-1); Clinton appointed a FEMA head, James Lee Witt from Arkansas, who sought to steer money toward the population and away from the presidency (Penny Bender, "FEMA Faulted for Not Preparing for Disasters," Gannett News Service, May 18, 1993).

134 Joseph Needham, *Science and Civilization*, vol. 6, pt. 2, 392, 403–4, 407. My thanks to Joe Scarry for directing me to China's granaries.

135 Ibid., 407.

136 Ibid., 411.

137 Derk Bodde, "Henry A. Wallace and the Ever-Normal Granary, *Far Eastern Quarterly* 5, no. 4 (August 1946), 413.

138 Needham, *Science and Civilization*, 417.

139 Pierre-Etienne Will and R. Bin Wong, *Nourish the People: The State Civilian Granary System in China, 1650–1850* (Ann Arbor: University of Michigan Press, 1991), 5, 25.

140 Ibid., 12, 528–32.

141 Ibid., 101.

142 Ibid., 14, 26, 33, 36, 57, 72–73.

143 Ibid., 104, 125.

144 Ibid., 47, 53, 104, 105, 125.

145 Clement Attlee, Public Records Office, CAB 130/41, GEN 253, 1st Meeting, 10 October 1948, cited in Hennessy, *The Secret State*, 124, 127.

146 This Box Hill is distinct from the Box Hill in Surrey where John Keats wrote *Endymion* and Jane Austen situated a key scene in *Emma*.

147 Hennessy, *The Secret State*, 171–77, 184–85. The list of those selected for shelter at Box Hill is contained in the 1963 Ministry of Defence War Book, declassified in 2000.

148 Ibid., xvii.

149 Hennessy interview with Sir Frank Cooper, BBC Radio 4, *Top Job*, August 8, 2000, cited in *The Secret State*, 180, 181.

150 Dr. Edgar Anstey of JIGSAW (Joint Inter-Services Group for the Study of All-Out Warfare), "Note on the Concept and Definition of Breakdown," June 1960, cited in Hennessy, *The Secret State*, 121. Anstey was a "Principal Scientific Officer from the Home Office" (143).

151 Epictetus, *Discourses*, in *Epictetus: The Discourses as Reported by Arrian, the Manual, and Fragments*, vol. 2, trans. W. A. Oldfather (Cambridge, MA: Loeb Classical Edition, 1985), 4.1.34.

152 Maurice Cranston, "The Political and Philosophical Aspects of the Right to Leave and to Return," in *The Right to Leave and to Return: Papers and Recommendations of the International Colloquium Held in Uppsala, Sweden, 19–20 June 1972*, ed. Karel Vasak and Sidney Liskofsky (Ann Arbor: University of Michigan Press, 1976), 21, 29.

153 It should also be noted that local communities *within* nuclear states, such as Oakland, CA, have sometimes attempted to establish right of exit by creating "nuclear free zones" that prohibit research, production, or transportation of nuclear weapons within the boundaries of their municipalities. In the case of Oakland, a federal court ruled that the ordinance violated the US Constitution's War Powers clause and, in effect, jeopardized national defense (*United States v. City of Oakland*, No. C–89–3305 JPV 13–14, Northern District of California, August 20, 1990, invalidating Oakland, California Ordinance 11,062 [December 16, 1988]). See Luis Li, "State Sovereignty and Nuclear Free Zones," *California Law Review* 79, no. 4 (July 1991), 1169–1204.

154 Andrew Mack, *Working Paper 1993/10: Nuclear Free Zones in the 1990s* (Canberra: Department of International Relations,

Research School of Pacific Studies, Australian National University, 1993), 17, 19.

155 Ibid., 8.

156 Ibid., 17.

157 Erik A. Cornellier, "In the Zone: Why the United States Should Sign the Protocol to the Southeast Asia Nuclear-Weapons-Free Zone," *Pacific Rim Law & Policy Journal* 12 (2003), 233, 234.

158 Jozef Goldblat, "Nuclear-Weapon-Free Zones: A History and Assessment," *Nonproliferation Review* (Spring/Summer 1997), 21.

159 See "Treaty on the Prohibition of the Emplacement of Nuclear Weapons and Other Weapons of Mass Destruction on the Sea-Bed and the Ocean Floor and in the Subsoil Thereof (1971 Seabed Treaty)," *Treaty Series* 955 (New York: United Nations, 1974), 117, note 9, available online at "Oceans in the Nuclear Age: Nuclear Free Zones," Law School, Berkeley, CA: http://www.law.berkeley.edu/centers/ilr/ona/pages/zones2.htm.

160 See "Overview" to "Oceans in the Nuclear Age," ibid., 9.

161 Cornellier, "In the Zone," 235–36.

162 Goldblat, "Nuclear-Weapon-Free Zones," 31. Goldblat enumerates eleven other ways in which the treaties are "deficient." For example, only Africa's Treaty of Pelindaba prohibits research on nuclear explosives (27, 31).

163 Gerrit Oakes cited in Navy Release, "Submarine Crew Accomplishes Mission, Earns Quals Doing Extended Patrol," November 16, 2008.

164 Secretary of the Navy Donald Winter cited in States News Service release, "1,000 Trident Patrols: SSBNs the Cornerstone of Strategic Deterrence," February 24, 2009.

165 Robert S. Norris, Hans M. Kristensen, Christopher E. Paine, *Nuclear Insecurity: A Critique of the Bush Administration's Nuclear Weapons Policies*, Natural Resources Defense Council, September 2004, 9, italics added.

166 Ibid., 6.

167 For a full account of the incompatible relation between the Second Amendment and nuclear weapons, see Elaine Scarry, "War and

the Social Contract: Nuclear Policy, Distribution, and the Right to Bear Arms," *University of Pennsylvania Law Review* 139, no. 5 (May 1991), 1257–1316.

168 Congressional "authorizations of force" (e.g., Korea) and "conditional" declarations (e.g., Gulf War) have neither the formal nor substantive properties of a declaration of war.

169 Bruno Tertrais, "The Last to Disarm? The Future of France's Nuclear Weapons," *The Nonproliferation Review* 14, no. 2 (July 2007), 258.

170 Such as Decree No. 64–46 (January 14, 1964) and Decree No. 96–520 (June 12, 1996) confining authority to engage nuclear forces to the president alone. See Born, "National Governance of Nuclear Weapons," 9; Tertrais, "The Last to Disarm?," 257; and Georg Nolte, *European Military Law Systems* (Berlin: De Gruyter Rechtwissenschaften Verlags, 2003), 292. Although as in other atomic-age democracies the requirement for a legislative authorization of war has been allowed to deteriorate, Nolte calls attention to a 1993 proposal by the Vedel Committee to strengthen Article 35 by amending it to require a parliamentary declaration of war for *any* military intervention outside French borders (294).

171 The "Subject Matter" of Article 246 is enumerated in a document that accompanies the Constitution, the Seventh Schedule, List I, numbers 1, 2, and 2A. India's constitution also includes environmental clauses on the obligation to protect wild animals, birds, and forests (Article 48A; Schedule 7, Clauses 17, 17A, 17B; Schedule 12, Clause 8) that may also one day contribute to an elimination of the country's nuclear weapons. Like the Swiss concern for the protection of the country's cultural heritage, the Indian constitution lists a positive duty "to value and preserve the rich heritage of our composite culture" (Part IVA, Article 51A).

Like many constitutions written after the invention of atomic weapons, the Indian constitution includes "emergency" provisions (Part XVIII) that potentially subvert other clauses in times of national crisis. In his study *Constitutional Dictatorship*, Clinton Rossiter reminds us that although these emergency clauses have become frequent in the nuclear age, they also antedate the era; he analyzes at length the emergency clause of Germany's Weimer Constitution that made possible Hitler's rise to unfettered executive power. For a rich comparative analysis of emergency provisions in a range of constitutions, see Bruce Ackerman's article in which he singles out the Canadian and South African constitutions as having the best safeguards ("The Emergency Constitution," *Yale Law Journal* 113, no. 5 [March 2004], 1029–91). More convincing, however, is Laurence Tribe and Patrick O. Gudridge's response to Bruce Ackerman arguing that *any* such emergency article—no matter how loaded with safeguards—carries a high risk of destroying the constitution ("The Anti-Emergency Constitution," *Yale Law Journal* 113, no. 8 [June 2004], 1801–70).

172 See, for example, in the UK parliament's online archive (www .parliament.uk), the House of Commons Public Administration Report, HC 422, of 2004 saying that Parliament's authorization of war should be required; and Clare Short, "Bill Requiring Parliament's Approval for Declaration of War and Dispatch of Troops," October 21, 2005.

173 State Department Press Release, "Background Notes: Pakistan," June 11, 2010.

174 See "E. Germans Deserting," *Newsday*, March 1, 1990, 12; *International Herald Tribune*, March 1, 1990, 1; Mark Trumbull, News Currents, *Christian Science Monitor*, March 1, 1990, 2.

175 Anatol Lieven and Mary Dejevsky, "Vilnius Anger Over Seizure of Deserters," *The Times* [London], March 28, 1990, 1.

176 Another area where we sometimes debate *whether* to aid rather than *how* to aid is the region of Good Samaritan laws. Many European countries have strict legal requirements for giving aid to strangers, whereas the Anglo-American tradition has (with the exception of a few weak state laws that have never been enforced) virtually none. But the debate centers on the question of legal enforcement, not the question of moral validity. No one questions the moral obligation to help someone in cases where doing so

brings no increased risk to oneself. For example, the standard air travel announcement about emergency oxygen begins, "If you are traveling with a child, or seated next to one . . ." In other words, if you are seated next to a child, you *are* traveling with one.

177 For example, the opening chapter of Locke's *Second Treatise* concludes, "*Political power*, then, I take to be a *right* of making laws with penalties of death . . . and in the defence of the commonwealth from foreign injury" (8). Later, in Section 88, Locke returns to the commonwealth's power to punish transgressions of the law, as well as "to punish any injury done unto any of is members, by any one that is not of it, (which is the *power of war and peace*;)" (47). The abiding background throughout both Hobbes and Locke is the state of non-injury.

178 The large gap between acting to diminish injury, on the one hand, and acting to inflict it, on the other, explains the distinct constitutional provisions for defense (where one is seeking to stop foreign invaders from injuring one's population) and offense (where one is actively inflicting harms on another country's population). If the home country is under attack, the president can, without consulting the population or Congress, *begin* to act to defend the nation because there is no ambiguity about whether human beings want the diminution of injury. Offensive wars, however, require full deliberation, hence a congressional declaration. There are, then, two release mechanisms on the act of injuring: the first is invasion; the second is a congressional declaration. The president becomes commander in chief if the country is invaded and (in the absence of an invasion) if Congress has declared war. Following the attack on Pearl Harbor on Sunday, December 7, 1941, Roosevelt began defense preparations even before going to Congress and asking for a formal declaration (Monday, December 8, 12:30 p.m.; Congress declared war at approximately 1:10 p.m.). In contrast, the United States was not under attack by Korea in 1950 (when Truman committed troops to the region), by Vietnam in 1962 (when the US began using Agent Orange) or in 1965

(when the US began carrying out continuous bombing raids), or by Iraq in August 1990 (when Bush Sr. sent troops) or January 1991 (when Bush Sr. initiated a major air strike) or 2003 (when Bush Jr. invaded Iraq). For a president to invade a country that has not attacked the US homeland without congressional authority was in each case illegal.

179 What happens if a law-abiding population finds that the state (in the name of emergency) has begun to inflict injury on those who are neither criminals nor enemies? Resistance to such a government will again draw on deep habits. During World War II, one remarkable village in southern France—Le Chabon—rescued thousands of Jewish children and adults. The actions of these Huguenot villagers were in part motivated by their long-practiced ethical commitment to what Philip Hallie calls "the preciousness of life" or what I have been calling the no-injury rule. But presumably many towns in Catholic France had just such an ethic of non-injury, yet they did not actively practice that ethic once the state legalized (and began to require cooperation in) the deportation of Jews. A second habit, Hallie shows, was at work in Le Chabon. As a result of being a minority religion in Catholic France, the inhabitants of the Huguenot village had at intervals across four centuries been subjected to persecution and had developed the practice of "refusing to abjure their faith." When Hallie conversed with the villagers about the aid they gave to Jews during the war, they declined to recognize their own acts as heroic or exceptional, instead regarding them as simply their way, their habit. See Philip P. Hallie, *Lest Innocent Blood Be Shed: The Story of the Village of Le Chabon and How Goodness Happened There* (New York: Harper Colophon, 1980), 167, 168, 172, 179.

Chapter Three: The Place of Habit in Acts of Thinking

1 For example, Aristotle, the Stoics, and the Christian fathers addressing spiritual exercises.

2 For example, John Locke, David Hume, and Bertrand Russell in Britain; William James and John Dewey in the United States.

3 For example, Pierre Bourdieu and Maurice Merleau-Ponty.

4 Montaigne, "Of Custom," in *The Complete Essays of Montaigne*, trans. Donald M. Frame (Stanford: Stanford University Press, 1965), 77, 78.

5 The indictment of habit is made by Beckett's Vladimir (late in *Waiting for Godot*), not by Beckett speaking in his own voice.

6 Aristotle, *Nichomachean Ethics,* in *The Complete Works of Aristotle: The Revised Oxford Translation*, ed. Jonathan Barnes, vol. 2, Bollingen Series LXXI (Princeton: Princeton University Press, 1984), 1737.

7 Thus T. L. Phipson reports that the French violinist and composer Charles Dancla was once offered a Stradivari violin for a performance, but after ten days of practice rejected it, finding the sound of the violin less beautiful than that produced by the nominally less valuable violin he had for many years used (*Famous Violinists and Fine Violins: Historical Notes, Anecdotes, and Reminiscences* [London: Chatto and Windus, 1896], 119).

8 William James, *Habit* (New York: Henry Holt & Co., 1914), 6. Italics in original.

9 Ibid., 11.

10 Ibid., 8.

11 Ibid., 66. James calculates that only before age twenty can we learn a language without a foreign accent (contemporary research has now pushed that age back to puberty), and between twenty and thirty we learn most professional and intellectual habits. Those, like Montaigne, who believe habit powerfully modifies perception in a negative direction will also be attentive to education, especially its negative outcomes: "I find that our greatest vices take shape from our tenderest childhood, and that our most important training is in the hands of nurses" (78).

12 Aristotle, *Nichomachean Ethics*, 1743.

13 John Dewey, *Human Nature and Conduct: an Introduction to Social Psychology* (New York: Henry Holt, 1922), 31. In *How We*

Think, Dewey suggests that what makes color particularly hard for a child is that unlike many other sensory events, it does not elicit from him a specific response or adjustment: "By rolling an object, the child makes its roundness appreciable; by bouncing it, he singles out its elasticity; by throwing it, he makes weight its conspicuous distinctive factor. . . . The redness or greenness or blueness of the object [in contrast] does not tend to call out a reaction that is sufficiently peculiar to give prominence or distinction to the color trait" (*The Middle Works of John Dewey 1899–1924.* vol. 6, ed. Jo Ann Boydston [Carbondale: Southern Illinois University Press, 1985], 275–76).

14 João Manuel Maciel Linhares et al., "The Number of Discernible Colors in Natural Scenes," *Journal of the Optical Society of America* 25, no. 12 (December 2008), 2918–24. My thanks to Bevil Conway for keeping me informed about evolving research on this question.

15 Dewey, *How We Think,* 215, 216.

16 Ibid., 223, 225, 263.

17 Dewey, *Human Nature and Conduct,* 100. So key a matter is sensory perception that James Ostrow, writing about the habitual in Merleau-Ponty and Dewey, titles the book *Sensitivity.* Ostrow sees the overwhelmingly negative connotations of habit for the modern period, and has the utopian hope that by renaming it he can bring about an appropriately positive view. The idea that we might actually begin to use the word "sensitivity" where we yesterday used the word "habit" seems extraordinary (Dewey himself only uses the word once or twice in *How We Think* and *Human Nature and Conduct*). But Ostrow's act of renaming at least reminds us how centrally interested in concrete sensation and sensitivity Dewey and Merleau-Ponty are.

18 Dewey, *How We Think,* 192, 212, 229, 230.

19 See Ronald Melzack, "Gate Control Theory: On the Evolution of Pain Concepts," *Pain Forum* 5, no. 1 (1996), 128–38, esp. 131; and Patrick D. Wall, "Comments After 30 Years of the Gate Control

Theory," ibid., 12–22, esp. 19. For preliminary findings suggesting that the neural architecture of pain may eventually have equivalents in other sensory events, see the analogue between phantom-limb pain in those missing a limb and phantom visual objects in those with eye damage (and with no cognitive impairment or psychopathology) in Geoffrey Schultz and Ronald Melzack, "Visual Hallucinations and Mental State: A Study of 14 Charles Bonnet Syndrome Hallucinators," *Journal of Nervous and Mental Disease* 181, no. 10 (1993), 639–43.

20 Edward Jablonski, *Gershwin* (New York: Doubleday, 1987), 8; jacket insert to *Gershwin Plays Gershwin: the Piano Rolls* (CD: Electra Nonesuch, 1993). Malcolm Gladwell describes the "10,000 hour rule" according to which great creative achievement in any field, whether music (e.g., the Beatles) or computer design (e.g., Bill Joy, Bill Gates), requires 10,000 hours of practice (*Outliers: The Story of Success* [New York: Little, Brown and Company, 2008], 35–68).

21 Tolstoy writes an instruction to himself in his diary on March 8, 1851: "Keep a journal of my weaknesses (a Franklin journal)"; and his entry for the days following are punctuated with italicized names of weaknesses ("*cowardly*," "*desire to show off*," "*lack of firmness*") followed by a specification of the discredited action. He also enumerates aspirations: "*Rule.* Try to form a style: (1) in conversation, (2) in writing." *Tolstoy's Diaries, Volume I: 1847–94*, ed. and trans. R. Christian (London: Athlone Press, 1885), 24, 25. For a rich account of Franklin's huge impact on Tolstoy as well many other eighteenth- and nineteenth-century Russian writers and scientists, see Eufrosina Dvoichenko-Markov, "Benjamin Franklin and Leo Tolstoy," *Proceedings of the American Philosophical Society* 96, no. 2 (April 21, 1952), 119–28; as well as Boris Eichenbaum's 1922 account of the direct link between Tolstoy's use of virtue charts in his diaries and his eventual achievement as a creative genius in *The Young Tolstoi*, trans. Gary Kern et al. (Ann Arbor: Ardis, 1972), 19–22.

22 D. H. Lawrence, "Benjamin Franklin," *Studies in Classic American Literature* (New York: Viking, 1923, 1964), 9, 14, 21.

23 Ibid., 13, 14, 16, 19, 21.

24 Ibid., 13, 19, 21.

25 Ibid., 11, 14, 19.

26 Franklin's glass harmonica, merely a curiosity today, was deeply admired in Franklin's own day, as evidenced by Mozart's last work of chamber music, the 1791 *Adagio and Rondo for Glass Armonica, Flute, Oboe, Viola, and Cello* (K. 617). Twenty years earlier, Mozart and his father (as we know from a September 21, 1771 letter from Leopold Mozart to his wife) stood on a balcony in Milan and waved to Marianne Davies, the first musician to play the glass harmonica in public and a young woman whose contact with Franklin was extensive enough that she has sometimes been (without sufficient evidence) identified as his niece; the Mozarts continued to meet with her both in Milan and in Venice (Emily Anderson, *Letters of Mozart and His Family Chronologically Arranged, Translated, and Edited with Introduction, Notes, and Indexes* [New York: Norton, 1985], 198). Leopold Mozart's letters to his wife also describe with admiration the glass harmonica owned by Dr. Franz Mesmer ("Wolfgang too has played upon it. How I should like to have one!"), whom he and his son often visited in Vienna during this period (letter of 12 August 1773, in *Letters of Mozart*, 236). Mesmer later used the instrument in his medical practice. Though Franklin would eventually be part of a scientific committee that wrote a formal report discrediting Mesmer's claims about the curative powers of magnetism, in 1779 he went to visit Mesmer in Paris because of the famous physician's interest in the glass harmonica (M. E. Grenander, "Reflections on the String Quartet[s] Attributed to Franklin," *American Quarterly* 27, no. 1, 82). Leopold was also acutely aware of Franklin's nonmusical achievements, as we know from his letter to his wife and son when they were in Paris in April 1778: "Write and tell me whether France has really declared war on England. You will

now see the American Minister, Dr. Franklin. France recognizes the independence of the thirteen American provinces and has concluded treaties with them" (*Letters of Mozart*, 525).

27 John R. Hale, *Lords of the Sea: The Epic Story of the Athenian Navy and the Birth of Democracy* (New York: Viking, 2009), 9.

28 Barack Obama, Forum with John Shattuck and Bob Herbert, John F. Kennedy Library, Boston, MA, October 20, 2006.

29 Robert C. Byrd, *Congressional Record–Senate*, 149, February 12, 2003, 3580, 3583.

30 Bill Clinton, interview with David Frost, *Talking with David Frost*, PBS, October 30, 1992: "Let me say something else. The other lesson of this war [in Vietnam] is if you're going to draft people and put them into combat, you should sell the conflict to the American people. You should get Congress to declare war. So there can be no doubt about what the objective is. And there ought to be clear and achievable objectives that you then put everything you've got behind achieving. None of those things happened in Vietnam. One of the things that it prepared me to do, and I think people who served in our generation—people like Senator John Kerry and Senator Bob Kerrey—I think all of us are determined to see that something like *that* does not happen again."

31 Joseph Story, *Commentaries on the Constitution of the United States: With a Preliminary Review of the Constitutional History of the Colonies and States Before the Adoption of the Constitution*, 4th ed. (Boston: Little, Brown, 1873), vol. 2, 87.

32 Locke, *Conduct of the Understanding*, 32.

33 Ibid., 124, 125.

34 Ibid., 93.

35 Montaigne, "Of Custom," 77.

36 Ibid., 83.

37 Dewey, *Human Nature and Conduct*, 58.

38 Ibid., 25.

39 Montaigne, "Of Custom," 83.

40 "The lawmaker of the Thurians ordained that whoever should

want either to abolish one of the old laws or to establish a new one should present himself to the people with a rope around his neck; so that if the innovation were not approved by each and every man, he should be promptly strangled" (ibid., 86).

41 Aristotle, *Nichomachean Ethics*, 1743.

42 Thomas Hobbes, *Leviathan*, ed. and introd. C. B. MacPherson (New York: Penguin, 1985), Pt. I, Ch. 6, 127. The alternative (and more widely credited) etymology of deliberation—which locates its root not in the word for "liberty" but the word for "weight"—also illuminates the materiality of the act. Two etymologists—Robert K. Barnhart and Ernest Klein—note that though "deliberation" originates in the root for "weigh," the formation of the word was influenced by the "liberty" root, an important point since scholars sometimes criticize Hobbes for his etymology. (See *The Barnhart Dictionary of Etymology* [New York: H. W. Wilson, 1988] and *A Comprehensive Dictionary of the English Language* [Amsterdam: Elsevier, 1971].)

43 Locke, *Conduct of the Understanding*, ed. Francis W. Garforth (New York: Columbia University Press, 1966), 100, 104, 105. Although Locke himself is a brilliant practitioner of similes, he complains that a simile acts as an accelerator used to trip thinking forward so that it can keep pace with speaking, leaping over ground that instead needs scrutiny.

44 Ibid., 87.

45 Ibid., 69, 89.

46 Ibid., 95, 124. Locke did not mean, however, that one should confine oneself to a single field of study. He urges what we today call cross-disciplinary work: "If men are for a long time accustomed only to one sort or method of thoughts, their minds grow stiff in it and do not readily turn to another. It is therefore to give them this freedom that I think they should be made to look into all sorts of knowledge and exercise their understanding in so wide a variety and stock of knowledge. But I do not propose it as a variety and stock of knowledge, but a variety and freedom of thinking, as an

increase of the powers and activity of the mind, not as an enlargement of its possessions"(73).

47 Ibid., 86, 87, 106. Italics added.

48 Ibid., 74, 75. "Clog" is here a wholly positive word, though it is at one later point used pejoratively (125).

49 Ibid., 123.

50 Dewey, *How We Think*, 188, 190.

51 Ibid., 189, 191.

52 Dewey, *Human Nature and Conduct*, 190.

53 Charles S. Peirce, "How to Make Our Ideas Clear," *Popular Science Monthly* (January 1878), 286–302, esp. 292. Though Peirce uses the word "thinking" throughout this essay, he clearly means that part of thinking that Aristotle calls "deliberating" since he repeatedly specifies that its goal is the taking of an action; and he excludes from "thinking" acts like listening to music that have no such action, acts which Aristotle identifies as "contemplation" or "perception" (see Chapter 1, page 8).

54 Dewey, *How We Think*, 189; Peirce, "How to Make Our Ideas Clear," 289.

55 Peirce, "How to Make Our Ideas Clear," 293.

56 The term is Peirce's, 292.

57 Jon Elster, *Ulysses and the Sirens: Studies in Rationality and Irrationality*, rev. ed. (Cambridge: Cambridge University Press, 1984), esp. 36–111.

58 Dewey, *How We Think*, 193, 194.

59 Elster, *Ulysses and the Sirens*, 43, 111.

60 Aristotle, *Nichomachean Ethics*, 1756.

ACKNOWLEDGMENTS

In creating the Global Ethics Series, Amnesty International and W. W. Norton express their conviction that the peoples of the earth not only share moral dilemmas but also share the ability to address those dilemmas transnationally. I am honored to write the first book for the series, and eager to read the other books that will soon follow.

My own conviction that nuclear weapons reside in a sphere of moral wrongdoing as absolute as torture began three decades ago when I was immersed in reading Amnesty International documents. So it is for me especially heartening to look at the fragile spine of this book and see *Thinking in an Emergency* in the company of Norton's wings and Amnesty's candle flame. The vision of those creating the Global Ethics Series—Kwame Anthony Appiah and Roby Harrington—has been inspiring. Across several years, Roby Harrington reappeared every few months to remind me of his dreams for this series. Step by ingenious step, Brendan Curry and Jake Schindel have translated my part in the dream into an actual published book. Allegra Huston gave scrupulous attention to copyediting, as did Mary Varchaver to the index. Warmest thanks, as always, to Amanda Urban for her careful and caring attention to each of my books.

Books sometimes have an oral life before a written life, and this book began at Yale Law School where, as a Leff Fellow, I gave a lecture and several seminars together entitled "Thinking in an Emergency." My deep thanks to that faculty, especially to Owen Fiss, Akhil Amar, and Bruce Ackerman. My research assistant at that time, Dan Buchanan, was a rich source of help, as Matthew Spellberg and Philip Francis have been more recently. Over the years, I have had the chance to speak about parts of the book to other law schools (USC, Stanford, Columbia, Cornell) and to humanities or ethics programs (Berlin's Freie Universität, University of Glasgow, Kings College at Cambridge, Dalhousie University, University of North Florida, and Harvard), from all of whose participants I have benefited. Spirited conversations with J. T. Scarry have recurred at regular intervals.

Long before I thought of this work as a freestanding book, Philip Fisher would ask about "Your book *Thinking in an Emergency*." He helped to bring the book into being simply by the force of his repeated questions. If I needed a personal exemplar of the principles of mutual aid described in the central chapter of this book, it would certainly be Philip Fisher who here, as in all my writing, provided breath, heartbeat, and shelter.

John Dewey says that "civilized man deliberately . . . sets up in advance of wreckage warning buoys and builds lighthouses where he sees signs that such events may occur." Philip Fisher and Eva Scarry—the beautiful woman to whom this book is dedicated—have long helped me understand the significance of Dewey's claim and the consequence of disregarding it.

INDEX